Ethics in Psychological Research

Sara Miller McCune founded SAGE Publishing in 1965 to support the dissemination of usable knowledge and educate a global community. SAGE publishes more than 1000 journals and over 800 new books each year, spanning a wide range of subject areas. Our growing selection of library products includes archives, data, case studies and video. SAGE remains majority owned by our founder and after her lifetime will become owned by a charitable trust that secures the company's continued independence.

Los Angeles | London | New Delhi | Singapore | Washington DC | Melbourne

Ethics in Psychological Research

A Practical Guide for the Student Scientist

Daniel P. Corts

Augustana College

Holly E. Tatum

Randolph College

Los Angeles | London | New Delhi
Singapore | Washington DC | Melbourne

FOR INFORMATION:

SAGE Publications, Inc.
2455 Teller Road
Thousand Oaks, California 91320
E-mail: order@sagepub.com

SAGE Publications Ltd.
1 Oliver's Yard
55 City Road
London EC1Y 1SP
United Kingdom

SAGE Publications India Pvt. Ltd.
B 1/I 1 Mohan Cooperative Industrial Area
Mathura Road, New Delhi 110 044
India

SAGE Publications Asia-Pacific Pte. Ltd.
18 Cross Street #10-10/11/12
China Square Central
Singapore 048423

Acquisitions Editor: Abbie Rickard
Editorial Assistant: Elizabeth Cruz
Production Editor: Kimaya Khasnobish
Copy Editor: Laurie Pitman
Typesetter: C&M Digitals (P) Ltd.
Proofreader: Ellen Howard
Indexer: Kathleen Paparchontis
Cover Designer: Michael Dubowe
Marketing Manager: Katherine Hepburn

Printed in the United States of America

ISBN: 978-1-5063-5000-4

This book is printed on acid-free paper.

18 19 20 21 22 10 9 8 7 6 5 4 3 2 1

BRIEF CONTENTS

DETAILED CONTENTS

PREFACE

Ethics in Psychological Research:
A Practical Guide for the Student Scientist

The idea for this book came from our personal experiences as mentors of undergraduate researchers as well as from situations our colleagues have encountered. We felt that there was no single source to help students and faculty navigate the difficulties they sometimes faced. We also realized that, in retrospect, had we discussed the pitfalls with student researchers *before* they began the research process, we might have avoided many of the problems. In searching for information to address ethical concerns that came up, for example on data ownership, it took many hours to track down the necessary information. Peer-reviewed articles often focus on one single topic in depth rather than on various issues related to ethical principles. There are websites, such as the Department of Health and Human Services' Office of Research Integrity website, that present basic information on the topic, but they are geared toward professional scientists. As it turns out, the best information we could find came from conversations with our peers at other colleges and universities. Their experiences had been the same, and they had worked through problems with their students in the same ways we had. Eventually, we realized that someone needed to gather the information in one place. We decided to take on that challenge and adopted the dual goals of (1) summarizing and teaching established ethical principles and (2) framing this in a way that would help student researchers think and behave ethically.

Ethics in Psychological Research is intended to be a practical guide for instructional purposes. Each chapter begins with a vignette describing an ethical dilemma. It would be easy for a reader to think of these as fiction, but we assure you that the scenarios and examples in the chapter openers (and throughout the chapters as well) come from our own experiences and from colleagues who generously shared their own stories with us. The chapters are structured much like the experience of a student and mentor working through the issues. Each opens with a student or professor facing an ethical issue. The chapter then provides a historical or philosophical background and followed by advice about how to approach or avoid the problem. Hopefully, you see the parallels. In life and in the book, we need context for more practical issues. This information is particularly important for students because an understanding of the basic ethical principles will allow them to tackle entirely new problems later on.

There are two sources that provide the majority of ethical principles for practically the entire book: the American Psychological Association and the U.S. federal government. In addition, each chapter focuses on a different set of ethical topics, and so the remaining source materials vary somewhat, including relevant scholarly work on the matter and organizations such as the American Statistical Association. In order to get the most out of the book, we ask that students and mentors go beyond the basic principles and think about how they apply to research situations both real and hypothetical. Real examples, such as the vignettes, are a good place to practice applying principles because you can get a sense for how researchers' motivations, aspirations, and beliefs can lead even the most ethical of researchers to lapse into questionable research practices (a term we introduce in Chapter 7). In addition to the vignettes, the discussion questions at the end of each chapter are structured to get you to think hypothetically: What if this situation occurred differently? What are other solutions? Why does this happen?

Ethical issues can be challenging, uncomfortable, and a drain on resources and emotions. Fortunately, most of them can be prevented by anticipating and preparing for them. We suggest having conversations at the level of the individual course or lab, the department, as well as across your campus. Policies can help solve problems if they do arise, and they certainly make it easier than doing what we did—usually that was coming up with a solution in the middle of a project. So, that is our advice: Educate yourself and plan ahead. And as a final word of encouragement, practicing sound ethics is every bit as important as sound methodology. When you get to the end of a project, you can be proud that you preserved integrity throughout the research process.

ACKNOWLEDGMENTS

There are two author names on this book, but it would not have happened without the encouragement and expertise of our editor, Abbie Rickard. We must also acknowledge her colleague at Sage, Reid Hester; this project never would have left the ground without his involvement. We are grateful for the contributions of a number of reviewers, listed, but we want to single out Beth Schwartz who played the role of super-reviewer. That job title may not have existed until now, but her quick, last-minute responses on the final round of revisions helped us gain confidence in our work before sending it to press.

The two of us spent over a year researching and writing this book, but, to be perfectly honest, it has been over 20 years in the making. We both began thinking about student research in our undergraduate years, but it was not until we met in graduate school that we began the conversation that eventually turned into this book. Reaching back that far, Dan must acknowledge the guidance from Lonnie Yandell and Pete Giordano who introduced him to research his junior year, and saw him through his first two conferences before earning his BS at Belmont University. Holly would like to acknowledge the late John Kibler who was her undergraduate research mentor at Mary Baldwin College and played a significant role in her attending graduate school in psychology. She would also like to acknowledge the contributions of her undergraduate research assistants, Shelby Koretke and Machaela Barkman, who offered invaluable assistance and feedback on the book chapters.

Dozens of other student researchers have contributed to this project as well, although most of them will never even realize it. It would be impossible to name them all, not to mention the difficulty in tracking down those who have long since graduated. Nonetheless, their contributions are meaningful, so a big thank you to all the students who have learned, hypothesized, and collected data with us. Thank you to those who sought advice, challenged us, and as a result, made us better mentors and researchers.

SAGE would like to thank the following reviewers for their input that shaped this text:

Gary Popoli, Stevenson University

Valerie Wilwert, Metropolitan State University

Stephanie A. Kazanas, Tennessee Technological University

Jordan R. Wagge, Avila University

ABOUT THE AUTHORS

DANIEL P. CORTS

Daniel P. Corts earned a PhD in Cognitive Psychology from the University of Tennessee and completed a postdoctoral fellowship in the teaching of psychology at Furman University. He has been at Augustana College for 17 years. Dan's work in supervising independent research, mentoring senior capstones, and bringing students into his lab has led to a number of publications and over 100 conference presentations. In addition, he works with various public, K–12 educational agencies to acquire and evaluate grants. These education projects have allowed Dan's students to see how the research methods they practice in the lab can be applied in practical situations as well. Dan is an active member of the Society for the Teaching of Psychology and recently completed his term as president of Psi Chi, the International Honor Society in Psychology. Dan's most significant publication experience is as coauthor of the introductory psychology text, *Psychological Science: Modeling Scientific Literacy* (Pearson) with Mark Krause. After a day of musing about methodology and ethics with his students, he enjoys spending time with his family where his kids, Jonah and Sophie, have proclaimed such topics off-limits.

HOLLY E. TATUM

Holly E. Tatum is the Mary Sabel Girard Chair in Psychology at Randolph College in Lynchburg, Virginia. She teaches undergraduate courses in experimental psychology, research methods, tests and measurements, gender, and health psychology, as well as the senior capstone course. Holly's research interests include health psychology and the scholarship of teaching and learning. Her recent work has examined the effect of different types of honor codes on academic integrity. As a proponent of undergraduate research, Holly has coauthored book chapters on research-based capstone courses and summer research programs for undergraduates. Holly regularly participates in the Randolph College Summer Research Program supervising undergraduates conducting research. She also involves students in her own research as assistants and collaborators. These projects have led to numerous presentations at national conferences, a book chapter, and three peer-reviewed journal articles with undergraduate coauthors. Holly earned her PhD in Experimental Psychology from the University of Tennessee.

ETHICS AND VALUES IN PSYCHOLOGICAL SCIENCE

At the end of her junior year, Meghan applied for a summer research grant at her university. To her surprise, the grant was funded. She was provided with a stipend and paired with a faculty mentor who provided her with expertise and equipment. Most of all, she was given free rein to design and conduct her first original experiment. The experience was a great opportunity to include in her medical school applications.

Interestingly, Meghan almost did not apply for the grant, despite encouragement from her Brain and Behavior professor who was quite impressed with her term paper on ethnic and gender differences in pain tolerance. "But, it's not like I can bring people to the lab and make them feel pain," Meghan had said. "There's no way that would be ethical." Her professor agreed, "No, you can't make them come in, but perhaps you could think of an ethical way to ask for volunteers and guide them through the experiment. Researchers do that all the time. How else do you think we have learned so much about how pain works?"

The scientific method is a profoundly powerful and versatile tool. In the relatively short period of history that it has been taught and practiced, life expectancy has increased, quality of life has improved, and our abilities to achieve new things and travel to new places have increased at a rate that was simply unimaginable a few centuries ago. In fact, the rate of technological advancement today was inconceivable even a few decades ago. The power of science—and what distinguishes it from other systems of thought—comes from its emphasis on objectivity and observation. Theories and hypotheses have scientific merit only to the extent that they generate testable predictions that are verified by data. Science requires us to set aside our personal opinions and assumptions, no matter how much we may want them to be true. Scientific findings can even challenge deeply held moral beliefs. No matter how effective science has been in explaining the world, there are those who interpret this objectivity as being cold and value-free, as if science is incompatible with conscience. That is simply not the case, and this book will demonstrate that science is actually built on and practiced with a set of values.

VALUES IN SCIENCE

What are scientific values? It is one thing to say that we, as students of a scientific discipline, value objectivity and observations. We would not have science without those, and that is why education includes courses on research methods, statistics, and laboratory techniques. However, there are other kinds of values in scientific endeavors; the kinds of values we will address in this book relate to concepts such as honesty, responsibility, and respect for the rights and well-being of the people or animals we study. These values are put into action through **research ethics**, *the principles used to define and promote acceptable behavior and discourage unacceptable behavior in scientific work.*

As Meghan's story illustrates, research ethics are often an extension of one's personal values. Even with limited training, Meghan realizes that she is facing some important ethical decisions. However, with experience comes an appreciation for how complex ethics can be and the fact that they encompass the entire research process. While Meghan considers the physical well-being of her volunteers, a lab group next door might be debating what to do with their data following a conference presentation, and her friend in the computer lab notices that, if he removes two unusual cases from his spreadsheet, he will have statistically significant results. Researchers with different levels of experience, motives, and opportunities may come up with different, even contradictory, answers if they rely solely on their gut feelings. This is why professionals across all scientific disciplines have set aside time to discuss, develop, and teach about ethics.

The purpose of this book is to introduce you to the ethics of research in psychological science. Although the values and principles addressed in this book are drawn from our experiences in psychology, the vast majority of these principles also apply to anyone conducting research—especially in fields like sociology, communications, exercise science, and many other subjects that make people the focus of their studies. Psychology and other disciplines have clinical and practical applications as well. There are ethics specific to psychotherapy, psychological assessments and testing, serving as an expert witness in court, and so on. Those principles are every bit as important as research ethics but are beyond the scope of this book. Our focus is on the **responsible conduct of research (RCR)**, *understanding and following the principles, rules, and guidelines for conducting research in an ethical manner* (Shamoo & Resnick, 2015). We will introduce you to research ethics through an examination of values rather than specific actions to take or to avoid. With these values as a foundation, each of the subsequent chapters will illustrate how they appear in the research process, the standards for preventing ethical problems, and ways to make ethical decisions as you conduct research yourself.

VALUES AND THE INTEGRITY OF RESEARCH

Most national governments have various agencies that fund scientific research. In the United States, the Department of Health and Human Services houses the Office of Research Integrity (ORI, see *Additional Resources* at the end of the chapter for more information). ORI establishes regulations and provides oversight of research within any organization or institution that receives research funding from the government. Most colleges and universities, whether public or private, receive some form of federal funds, such as grants for research, training opportunities, or equipment. Therefore, they are obligated to follow the regulations put forth by ORI. For example, you will read in Chapters 4 and 5 that institutions must have committees review and approve research on human subjects. In addition to setting these rules and regulations, ORI investigates allegations of misconduct while also promoting integrity through education on RCR. It seems favorable to emphasize "good citizenship" among researchers (Steneck, 2007), rather than focus on strict warnings and harsh punishments. Therefore, ORI proposes that the responsible conduct of research is best thought of as a commitment to a set of shared values:

- *Honesty*: conveying information truthfully and honoring commitments

- *Accuracy*: reporting findings precisely and taking care to avoid errors

- *Efficiency*: using resources wisely and avoiding waste

- *Objectivity*: letting the facts speak for themselves and avoiding improper bias (Steneck, 2007, p. 3)

This is not a complete list, but it is a good place to emphasize that scientific values are not simply nice concepts to think about, nor are they just ways for researchers to be polite. These values are necessary for scientific knowledge to progress, as we will see with the value of openness.

OPEN SCIENCE

The concept of openness, related to honesty and accuracy described above, promotes more effective research in a number of ways but largely because it facilitates **replication**, *repeating research methods with different investigators in different locations to test whether the same results are observed*. Replication benefits science in several ways, such as identifying Type I errors, which you may have learned about in a statistics course. These type I errors, also called *false positives* occur when a statistical test produces significant results, but the results are actually due to random error. It is very difficult to detect a Type I error in a single study. However, if research findings can be replicated, it makes Type I errors seem less likely. Finally, replication can be used to detect experimenter effects such as carelessness, a misconception about the use of techniques or methods, and even outright dishonesty. Whatever the reason, research that does not replicate is likely to have less impact.

Despite the importance of replication, historically it has not been practiced in psychology, or in any other fields for that matter. This is largely the product of two connected factors: how scientific journals select what to publish and how university administrators evaluate their faculty. To a large extent, deans and department chairs expect their faculty to publish research frequently to be awarded tenure, get promoted, and earn merit pay. Meanwhile, editors want to publish new, statistically significant findings to elevate the status of their journal. Because editors are not looking for replications of previously published research, faculty have little motivation to spend time on it. In fact, it can cost faculty by occupying time and resources that could be spent trying to produce the new findings editors are seeking. As a consequence, scientific disciplines have not been efficient at weeding out false positives, experimenter effects, and dishonesty.

The concern over replication has led to a recent movement in psychology to openly share data so that other scientists can confirm or replicate the findings. In 2014, the Center for Open Science (COS) was created to promote three core values in science: *openness*, *integrity*, and *reproducibility* (Nosek, 2017, p. 6). Their mission is to change the culture of scientific practices to an open science framework where researchers collaborate on projects by sharing data and other important components of their research—these are covered in much more detail in Chapters 8 and 9. In short, by using larger data sets and including many different samples from multiple settings, scientists can test the strength of the overall effect and the reproducibility of their findings.

It is somewhat ironic that an effort to encourage replication has led to what some call the **replication crisis**, *the concern among a large number of scientists (led by psychologists) that many—perhaps even most—peer-reviewed studies cannot be reproduced by other researchers*. This arose from a project initiated by founders of the COS in which dozens of researchers around the world went about replicating 100 published studies in psychology, including both experimental and correlation studies (Open Science Collaboration, 2015). Many were surprised to learn that only 36% of these replication studies reproduced the original results. Naturally, there may be good reasons why so many studies failed to replicate, and it may be that some of the replication studies themselves produced errors. Regardless, openness in science is an example of how the values driving ethical principles are not just nice, they are necessary.

PSYCHOLOGISTS' CODE OF ETHICS

The American Psychological Association's (APA) *Ethical Principles of Psychologists and Code of Conduct* (2016) are standards of behavior for psychologists in their professional practice, which may include any combination of teaching, research, supervision, consulting, program design and administration, and counseling and clinical work. The code is based on five broad principles—the values underlying all psychological work, as shown in Table 1.1.

Understanding these five principles helps psychologists identify situations in which ethical issues may arise and then consider ways of preventing issues or resolving problems. We have already encountered some of these principles in Meghan's situation. She had the intuitive sense that she should not cause harm, and that people of various backgrounds are likely to experience the same painful stimuli differently. Rather than relying on her intuitions, Meghan can actually turn to the APA ethics code to find that her concerns relate to nonmaleficence and her respect for people's rights and dignity.

TABLE 1.1 ■ The APA's Ethical Principles and Code of Conduct	
Principles	**Definition**
Beneficence and Nonmaleficence	Psychologists will promote well-being (*beneficence*) and avoid doing harm (*nonmaleficence*).
Fidelity and Responsibility	Psychologists uphold trusting relationships within their community and working relationships.
Integrity	Psychologists will behave with honesty and truthfulness in all professional activities.
Justice	Psychologists should treat others with fairness. This includes recognizing their personal biases and the limits to their expertise.
Respect for People's Rights and Dignity	Psychologists must work to protect the rights of individuals (privacy, confidentiality, autonomy) and respect cultural differences to avoid prejudices.

With experience, psychologists find themselves working in a variety of situations with more nuances than five broad principles can address in any detail. Therefore, the ethical principles are further codified in 10 *Ethical Standards*. These standards are directives, describing how the principles should be addressed in practice. For research psychologists, Meghan included, avoiding harm and respecting dignity can both be seen in standards relating to *informed consent* (a central topic of Chapter 4); psychologists must communicate and document that they have obtained permission from the individual participants in their studies. Similarly, psychologists prevent harm and demonstrate respect by providing anonymity and confidentiality as much as possible, thereby preventing potentially embarrassing or damaging information from becoming public.

The APA's *Ethical Principles of Psychologists and Code of Conduct* can be found online (see *Additional Resources* at the end of this chapter). As we move through each chapter, we will identify the principles and standards that will best inform each ethical dilemma or scenario. We will rely on both the APA's ethics code as well as general research values identified by ORI and other organizations. An important set of values to consider are those related to collaborations with others.

ETHICS AND THE STUDENT SCIENTIST

The ethics of psychological research are universal: We expect colleagues, students, and mentors to understand and abide by the same set of principles. Nonetheless, there are some differences in how ethics might be applied in contexts where only professionals are involved, when the project is entirely conceived and conducted by students, and, perhaps most commonly, when students and their mentors work together. Consider the following research scenarios:

- An I/O (industrial/organizational) psychologist examines whether employee substance abuse problems might contribute to dishonesty in the workplace.

- A neuroscientist exposes laboratory rats to extreme stress, then dissects the brains to examine changes in brain volume.

- After completing data collection, a cognitive psychologist finds that his statistical tests fall just short of significance. He decides to eliminate an outlier or two from his data and runs the same test again, this time getting statistical significance.

Do these represent ethical problems? Does it make a difference if the researcher is a student rather than a professor? In each case, it is worthwhile to answer both questions. For the I/O psychologist, it is possible to collect data from a wide range of people in many different locations, thereby making anonymity very easy to achieve. In contrast, imagine a student at a liberal arts college who does not have the same resources and professional contacts. Her project is more likely to involve a survey of her peers. At a small college, she will have to go through a much more sophisticated process to ensure she does not inadvertently discover the identity of someone with a substance abuse problem or a history of cheating. This could even mean sacrificing the quality of the research by eliminating personally identifying questions about race, gender, major, and year in school. In these two situations, we see that the same ethical principles apply, but they call for somewhat different methods of implementation.

It is not necessarily the case that all student research requires a different approach to ethics, but we believe it is well worth the effort to consider each study individually and before they are underway. For the neuroscientist, the use of lab animals in this way requires a strong likelihood of significant medical advances. That holds true when a student assistant is in the lab, but is far less likely if the research is proposed for a student's independent capstone project. For the psychologist manipulating his data set, that is a dubious practice no matter what the researcher's status is.

There are many different stages in the research process, and so there are many varieties of research principles to understand and follow. Despite this complexity, there is a relatively simple set of steps for viewing ethics from the perspective of the student scientist. We call these steps the PASA model, and we encourage students and mentors to work through these steps together before embarking on any research project.

Principles. Make sure all participating individuals understand the ethical principles that are involved in the project, including the ethics of working with human subjects, managing and storing data, writing and reporting results, and so on. Without a solid understanding of the principles, it would be difficult for anyone to complete an ethical project, whether a student or a professor.

Assumptions. People often make assumptions about proposed research that, if mistaken, may lead to a violation of ethical principles. It is imperative that students, collaborators, and mentors understand and address those assumptions. For example, imagine an individual on an ethics review committee who is asked to approve the neuroscientist's study described earlier. The proposal would include the details of treating and euthanizing lab animals, and it would be easy to assume that the neuroscientist is knowledgeable, competent, and honest enough to follow the ethical principles. However, that assumption would no longer hold if student lab assistants have been poorly trained and left unsupervised.

Status of the researcher. Next, examine how those assumptions might be challenged by the presence of a student on the research team, or when the student is acting as an independent researcher. Obviously, students are unlikely to have the same level of competence and experience as a professor, especially in the case of the neuroscientist. Moreover, students are less likely to have the resources and contacts to collect data at workplaces around the country, as in the example of the substance abuse research. Students may not be aware of the ethics of conducting and reporting statistical analyses, simply because learning the procedures themselves can be challenging and take time.

Adapt the rules to fit the context. With a full understanding of the principles, assumptions, and the unique situations involving students, you should be able to establish a set of guidelines to ensure ethical behavior. Again, the values and principles remain the same, but may be addressed in different ways. For the substance abuse research, the student may have to ask fewer questions to avoid the potential to identify individual participants. Ethics review committees may ask for evidence that the lab assistants are fully qualified; perhaps a certificate of completing an ethics course or proof that they each completed a prerequisite lab course. For a student learning about statistical analyses, it might actually be OK to manipulate the data if (and only if) the research context is purely to help the student learn about the consequences of various practices. In each example, the context makes a huge difference.

LOOKING FORWARD

So far in this chapter, we have seen that the objectivity of science serves to keep individuals' beliefs, hopes, and assumptions in check. However, science is far from a value-free enterprise. Our values are spelled out in the ethical guidelines we follow and reflected in our behavior toward others, ranging from people who volunteer to participate in studies to the community who stands to benefit from our efforts. The purpose of this book is to help you confidently engage in the responsible conduct of research.

When you look at the table of contents, you will see that the book is laid out to address all of the steps in the research process in roughly the same order that researchers encounter them, particularly the chapters on protecting human subjects, gaining IRB (Institutional Review Board) approval, data analysis, and writing up research results. Other topics are not necessarily steps in the research process but focus more on the environment in which research occurs. That is the case in Chapter 2 in which we consider academic freedom and supervision; these topics include questions of what rights and responsibilities go along with being a student researcher or mentor. Within each chapter, you will likely notice the same underlying structure. Each chapter begins with a vignette that illustrates a type of ethical decision or conflict. These are actual events that have occurred with our own students or with students that our colleagues have supervised at other colleges and universities. You will learn about the values and ethical principles that are the focus of the chapter, and see how they can be applied to various research activities. Finally, each chapter includes how the principles may vary according to the context and, in several chapters, guides student researchers through the ethical decision-making process.

Chapter Summary

- Scientists engage in the responsible conduct of research by establishing, teaching, and practicing research ethics.

- The Office of Research Integrity bases its work on four key values: Honesty, Accuracy, Efficiency, and Objectivity.

- The Center for Open Science emphasizes the three values of openness, integrity, and reproducibility. The center has demonstrated that these values are not just matters of behavior, they are fundamental to the development of knowledge in any discipline.

- The American Psychological Association has established a code of conduct based on the five principles of *beneficence* and *nonmaleficence*, *fidelity* and *responsibility*, *integrity*, *justice*, and *respect for people's rights and dignity*.

- Research ethics are universal: Everyone engaged in psychological research is expected to follow the same rules whether they are undergraduates or senior faculty members with tenure.

- Despite the universality of research ethics, being a student puts you in a unique position. In order to ensure ethical behavior for student researchers, students and mentors may apply the PASA model to their project before the project begins.

- The PASA model addresses four things: understanding the principles, examining assumptions, considering the status significance of having a student researcher, and making adaptations to fit the context.

Discussion Questions

1. The Office of Research Integrity describes four values important to scientific research. The Center for Open Science names three. To what extent do these two organizations identify the same underlying values, despite using different names for them? In what ways do their values differ?

2. Consider the principles of *fidelity* and *responsibility* as you read this scenario:

   Avery showed up late for the lab group meeting today, and once again, his assigned work was sloppy and incomplete. That makes the third time in the past five meetings. Today, he was supposed to arrive with edited photocopies of an informed consent document for research participants. Not only did he fail to make copies, but the supervising professor had to make additional edits before printing the document. She let Avery know very clearly that he is no longer just slowing down his group's progress, he is actually beginning to harm their work.

   a. How do the values of fidelity and responsibility relate to Avery's behavior in this example? Can any other APA values be used to address Avery's behavior?

3. Think about the principles of *beneficence* and *nonmaleficence* in the following scenario.

    Dr. Ortiz has enrolled one of his strongest students, Camille, in an honors research practicum for juniors. Although he is confident she will do an excellent job, he does have a big concern. Namely, honors students are to generate ideas for their senior theses based on their practicum, and then design and conduct their own study their senior year. Dr. Ortiz wonders exactly what an undergraduate—even a very accomplished one—should attempt when it comes to a topic like suicide. Should students be allowed to conduct research on such a sensitive topic, and with volunteers who could potentially be in crisis?

    Using the guide below, apply the PASA model to help Dr. Ortiz translate the principles of *beneficence* and *nonmaleficence* to student researchers.

    A. Principles. Think about your expectations for researchers working with individuals who have suicidal thoughts. What are some specific ways they might incorporate *beneficence* when designing a study, or act on it when gathering data? How about *nonmaleficence*?

    B. Assumptions. To address the principles in the ways you described, Dr. Ortiz must have certain traits, knowledge, skills, and credentials. What are some of these qualities?

    C. Status. Are any of these qualities unlikely to apply to an undergraduate like Camille? If so, how would that affect her ability to engage in the same behaviors you identified in A, above?

    D. Adapt. Considering the differences between the professor and the student, how might you adapt the expectations you set in A, above? Are there any restrictions or additional actions you would suggest?

Additional Resources

American Psychological Association

The APA is the largest professional organization for psychology. Their ethics code is very influential in this book. If you would like to read sections of it for yourself, it is freely available at http://www.apa.org/ethics/code/

Office of Research Integrity

ORI provides a vast collection of resources. Perhaps the best place to start is with the e-book, *Introduction to the Responsible Conduct of Research*, quoted earlier. It is available in a web version or as a downloadable file at https://ori.hhs.gov/ori-intro

The main web page will give you a look at all of the resources, including cases of research misconduct, videos, and infographics. https://ori.hhs.gov/

Center for Open Science

You can visit the COS website to learn more about the work they do to improve the scientific process: https://cos.io/

Their flagship project is known as the Open Science Framework. This is a web-based system that helps scientists manage the workflow of their research in a way that encourages replication and the sharing of data and other resources.

References

American Psychological Association. (2016). *Ethical principles of psychologists and code of conduct*. Retrieved from http://www.apa.org/ethics/code/

Nosek, B. A. (2017, March 6). *Center for open science: Strategic plan*. Retrieved from https://osf.io/x2w9h

Open Science Collaboration. (2015). Estimating the reproducibility of psychological science. *Science, 349*(6251). Retrieved from http://science.sciencemag.org/content/349/6251/aac4716

Shamoo, A. E., & Resnick, D. B. (2015). *Responsible conduct of research* (3rd ed.). New York, NY: Oxford University Press.

Steneck, N. H. (2007). *Introduction to the responsible conduct of research*. Washington, DC: Office of Research Integrity. Retrieved from https://ori.hhs.gov/sites/default/files/rcrintro.pdf

2

UNDERSTANDING FREEDOMS AND RESPONSIBILITIES

Kia is completing a senior capstone project under the supervision of a tenure-track assistant professor. Now at the halfway point, she has surveyed significant amounts of literature arguing that the consumption of hardcore pornography has significant undesirable effects; it has been correlated with lower satisfaction in sexual relationships as well as increased verbal and physical aggression. However, these arguments are based on correlational data that are consistent with, but weak evidence for, causality. To test for a causal effect of pornography, Kia proposed a clever, well-designed experiment using established methods of social-cognitive psychology. During the IRB process, the university's administration learned of the proposal, became concerned that the study might affect the reputation of the university, and instructed the supervising professor to stop the project immediately.

Kia's experience brings up questions about **academic freedom**, *the rights for members of an academic community to research, teach, and speak publicly without official interference or threat of punishment.* The principles comprising academic freedom allow scholars to pursue ideas that may be scientifically valid, even if those topics are controversial or unconventional. For the same reason, university administrators have an ethical responsibility to protect their faculty's freedoms. Although academic freedom allows faculty to research and teach topics that may be controversial, there is also an ethical responsibility to use it for advancing scientific knowledge, not personal agendas. History is filled with examples of major scientific advances that were nearly thwarted by authorities. For example, in the 17th century, Galileo was threatened and imprisoned by leaders of the Catholic Church and his university for arguing that the earth orbited the sun. Galileo's work not only challenged scientific fact, but the very way science operated in society. Naturally, we do not set the standards quite that high for our students—or ourselves, for that matter—but we still must ask how academic freedom applies. We typically assume that academic freedom would protect a professor researching a taboo subject, but is the same true for students? Does Kia have the protections of academic freedom to pursue an experiment on pornography?

Conflicts about academic freedom sometimes arise from having multiple perspectives regarding a student's independent research; the student, mentor, and university each have an interest in the student's work. As Kia's case illustrates, those perspectives can be very different. The student may see the research as a chance to explore personal interests and reach an early career milestone. The mentor may come away with a sense of pride or frustration, depending on the student's work ethic and abilities. The university may use this as a chance to publicize a success story to the community and to potential students, or as a potential risk (e.g., the administration fears that outsiders will see this as promoting pornography on campus). Additionally, this example illustrates how a failure to have clear policies can lead to significant disappointment and a loss of productivity; after all, Kia's month-long literature review may have gone to waste.

In this chapter, we will first discuss academic freedom in more detail before turning to the student–mentor relationship. Both of these topics address aspects of the research process that should be established before work gets underway. Imagine how different Kia's experience would have been if the university had an established policy outlining the limits they would place on students' academic freedom? Kia certainly would have had a more positive experience, and would have been able to devote much more time to a project she could see to its completion.

ACADEMIC FREEDOM

The modern concept of academic freedom was formalized by the American Association of University Professors (AAUP) in its publication, *1940 Statement on Academic Freedom and Tenure* (AAUP, 1940). In this document and subsequent statements, the AAUP argued that academic freedom was not just a benefit to faculty, but an absolutely essential part of academic work. The AAUP's definition of academic freedom includes three main principles, each representing a different aspect of academic life:

1. As researchers, faculty have "full freedom" to pursue the questions they see as important and relevant to their disciplines. Research programs should be determined by the likelihood that they will advance knowledge, not serve personal or institutional agendas.

2. As teachers, faculty are free to select the disciplinary topics they feel are most important for their students while omitting other material. They are free to choose the assignments and pedagogy that, in their professional judgment, are best suited to help their students learn about the discipline.

3. As citizens of a democratic society, faculty have the freedom—some would argue the responsibility—to speak as individuals without representing their institutions. This is particularly useful when an expert has a personal opinion on a topic for which the university has no particular stance, such as a professor of educational psychology sharing his research on the benefits of arts education to a local school board facing budget cuts.

The principles that comprise academic freedom are broadly defined to cover multiple activities across the entire range of disciplines. For behavioral scientists, the most relevant application of academic freedom tends to be *intellectual freedom*. That is to say that a psychologist has the right to research and write about any topic in that discipline, even if it is likely to be offensive to some. As an example, imagine Kia's advisor, Dr. Ahuja, had designed the experiment on pornography as part of his own program of research. If the administration challenged him, he could argue that he was protected by academic freedom and that the administration was clearly in the wrong. In fact, the AAUP may very well appeal to the university on Dr. Ahuja's on behalf. Professor Ahuja could also claim to have *sociopolitical freedom*; an expert can share evidence from his discipline to argue for or against policies, such as a city council debating whether or not to relax restrictions on adult-themed businesses. Note that this type of activity is not research, but rather a logical, sociopolitical extension of one's expertise. Finally, Dr. Ahuja's fine arts colleagues enjoy *artistic freedom*. A creative writing instructor can write sexually explicit fiction, or a drawing professor may sketch nude figures, or even have a nude model posing for a class. While neither of these artistic examples are considered pornography in most communities, individuals or small groups may and sometimes do try to suppress such activities, describing them as obscene. If the university follows the AAUP's recommendations, all of these activities are likely to be protected.

Models of Academic Freedom for Students

Earlier, we recommended that academic freedom standards be formalized for student-led research, perhaps at the level of the academic department or the university. The question raised by Kia's experience is not just whether there should be a formal policy but, also, what should that policy be? To answer this question, we assume the university's administration and faculty have an understanding of any limitations faculty might face along with the consequences of misconduct or abuses of that freedom. With the mentor's position clarified, a policy for students can be crafted to reflect any additional conditions or restrictions that may apply at the undergraduate and graduate levels. To facilitate this process, we propose three approaches to student freedom that may be adopted as models. Note that in each of these models, we assume that the students are more than just research assistants; they are making some contribution to the development and planning of the study, and may even be the principal investigator.

The *full-freedom model* is the broadest approach to student academic freedom and grants students the same status as tenured, full professors at their university. This means that as long as the students can figure out how to conduct an experiment, they can do it without threat of punishment or penalty. The *limited-freedom model* is at the opposite end of a spectrum from full-freedom, and probably is applicable only to faculty-student collaboration. This would have the university place restrictions on student freedoms, which could potentially limit a mentor's ability to conduct his own research if a student collaborator was involved. The most reasonable approach appears to be the middle path, which may be called the *developmental-freedom model*. Students must earn the trust of their mentors, who have the most say about what and how they research. Because mentors are faculty and are protected by academic freedom, they are responsible for determining what the student is capable of and how successful the research might be. Therefore, the professor's status might be considered a proxy for the student. In Kia's case, this means that the if the mentor approves of Kia's research, then the administration should never get involved.

Although the protections of academic freedom are ultimately the responsibility of the university, it begins with effective student–mentor relationships. Quality mentoring relationships help student researchers understand how social and personal factors outside the lab can still have a profound effect on the research process.

Responsible Working Relationships

Research mentors have always been a part of doctoral education where a significant research project is required. More recently, evidence for the benefits of research in undergraduate education has led to calls from various groups to make research a key part of science curricula (Kuh, 2008; Lopatto, 2006). It is probably not surprising to learn that the degree and types of benefit students get out of their research experience depends a great deal on the quality of mentoring (Kuh, 2008; Linn, Palmer, Baranger, Gerard, & Stone, 2015). Student–mentor relationships are key to successful student research from the moment they are formed; and, like academic freedom, it is best to establish expectations even before the research begins. Naturally, mentoring continues through the end of the study when the presentations or publications have been completed and the data properly stored. There is no reason that the mentoring relationship must end there and, in fact, many young faculty remain in touch with their mentors from their undergraduate and graduate years.

To begin, we should distinguish between mentorship and collaboration. Mentoring, the subject of this chapter, typically involves at least two roles. First, a mentor fosters the development of the knowledge, skills, and ethics relative to the discipline and, particularly for graduate students, the profession. The mentoring does not necessarily involve direct instructions on what or how to research, as that would be considered teaching. Instead, the role of mentor is more about providing support in terms of expertise and resources. Second, mentors should be professional role models outside of the laboratory. As Kia's case illustrates, research is affected by factors completely beyond what is covered in research methods courses. Students also benefit from guidance related to personal growth, such as dealing with interpersonal conflict or failures in the lab. Collaboration includes activities in which two researchers work together, both contributing substantially to a project. With that in mind, it does not even have to include a mentor; collaborations can involve two or more student researchers. For that reason, we will focus on mentoring in this chapter and turn to collaboration in Chapter 3.

Because mentoring is about personal and professional development, the student's interests should be considered primary. Students have the most to learn—not just the methods and techniques of the laboratory, but responsible and ethical behavior we hope they will practice in their own work. Although this chapter focuses on the student as principal researcher, the same is true of research assistants who often benefit from the mentorship of their employer. As for mentors, they serve as examples of how to conduct research. If the mentors teach and model appropriate ethics, the students are more likely to know how to make the right choices later on, and will be more likely to follow through with the protocol. It follows that ethical behavior requires a team to work together, communicate well, and ensure that all individuals understand and complete assigned tasks. This connection leads us to summarize the ethics of working together with two ideas: mutual respect and the acknowledgment of multiple relationships (Anderson & Shore, 2008).

Ethics in Mentoring

The concept of **multiple relationships** reflects the fact that *students and mentors interact in different contexts with different roles* (APA, 2017). A student's roles may include working as a research assistant or teaching assistant, a student in the mentor's courses, and a protégé completing a senior or master's thesis. For graduate students in particular, mentors are more likely to form personal relationships that last well into the student's career—especially if it is an academic career (Anderson & Shore, 2008). Although the term *multiple relationships* originated in clinical fields—for example, a therapist should not become a personal friend of a patient outside of therapy—it also applies in the context of research. Imagine a student who commits an honest mistake in the lab, costing the mentor a chance to present the results at a major conference. If that student then has an exam in the professor's class, it sets up a situation in which the professor may treat the student differently, even if it is not a conscious act.

Multiple relationships create opportunities for two people to affect each other in many ways, both positive and negative. For this reason, and others, the student–mentor relationship must be based in *mutual respect*. The mentor should be aware that the student will need instruction and supervision, time to complete coursework and meet other obligations, and to take care of basic personal needs. The student should realize that the mentor is a busy person, too, and must schedule around classes, grading time, and, in many cases, family life. Interestingly, many undergraduates report that they have never considered these issues before, although they are clearly sympathetic once they do (Campbell & Campbell, 2000).

A principle as broad as *mutual respect* is important and can certainly help with ethical decision making. However, there is an approach to mentoring relationships that we find extremely helpful, and it based on five distinct and more-specific constructs. The first four of these were first introduced in Chapter 1: *beneficence, nonmaleficence, fidelity,* and *justice*. Here, we add the fifth one, *autonomy* (Barnett, 2008).

Beneficence is the responsibility to provide help and to have one's actions benefit the other. Mentors should help students identify talents, interests, and opportunities.

Nonmaleficence is the responsibility to avoid behaviors that have negative consequences. Mentors should be mindful of their power. Because they might assign grades and offer recommendations or job references, students may be afraid to say no to requests from a mentor, particularly personal requests or invitations that do not involve the research itself. Students also have responsibilities: They must realize that their behaviors can have negative effects, such as placing heavy demands on a mentor's time and resources, or damaging a mentor's reputation through academic dishonesty or presenting poor-quality work.

Fidelity means individuals should carry out their roles faithfully. For mentors, it is important to provide opportunities and guidance for the student to grow. It is not faithful to the mentoring role to leave students without assignments or instructions in the lab. Students fulfill their roles when they seek and follow constructive feedback and advice.

Justice, in this context, means that individuals should be treated fairly and given the same considerations. Like autonomy, this factor relies more heavily on the mentor's actions. For example, if there is a unique opportunity for student–faculty collaboration, the mentor should be open to considering all students, and then selecting individuals based on qualifications and interests. Notice that justice does not mean awarding everyone the same opportunity, but it does mean focusing on merit, experience, and professional interests rather than on who has a good social connections or who might be a little annoying interpersonally.

Finally, **autonomy** is *the ability to make one's own decisions and act accordingly.* This factor requires the mentor to provide instructions and opportunities to students, with increasing responsibility over time. As students gain competence, they will benefit a great deal from identifying and solving problems on their own. Students, on the other hand, need to develop and exercise autonomy as they progress. If you forget how to conduct a factorial ANOVA, you may demonstrate autonomy by referring to a statistics textbook or looking up any of the dozens of free instructional videos online. Of course, students should go to mentors for help, but it is worth finding out what you can do on your own and what you need to practice.

It would be impossible to catalog every single type of interaction a student and mentor might experience. Nonetheless, these five principles are very flexible and can be applied to just about any situation imaginable. As is the case with academic freedom, difficulties arise when expectations are not clear at the outset, so we recommend establishing those when first meeting.

The commonalities of academic freedom and student–mentor relationships may not be obvious, but after close examination, you should see that both rely on mutual respect and require individuals and institutions to look out for everyone's best interests. In addition, when expectations are not clear, it is easy for conflicts to arise and, in some cases, become very serious. This risk can be greatly reduced by thoughtful conversations and well-designed policies that happen before the student's research ever begins.

Chapter Summary

- Academic freedom is the principle that allows researchers to study topics that they believe are important to their discipline. It does so by preventing colleagues and administrators from obstructing work or penalizing researchers for having controversial ideas.

- There are no broadly recognized standards for how academic freedom applies to student research, but we suggest having policies in place to guide students and mentors before work begins.

- We offered three models of academic freedom for students. Developmental freedom may work best, because this allows the mentor to set the standards based on the student's abilities and record of responsible behavior.

- Students and mentors should be mindful of two main principles: multiple relationships and treating each other with mutual respect.

- It is wise to discuss responsibilities and expectations of students and mentors as soon as the relationship is formed.

- Decisions about behavior should be made with five themes in mind: *beneficence*, *nonmaleficence*, *fidelity*, *autonomy*, and *justice*.

Discussion Questions

1. This chapter introduces the concept of academic freedom with a brief description of its history and purpose. Do you think academic freedom is as relevant to you as a student as it is for your professors? Which model of academic freedom for students do you think is most suitable, or would you come up with a model of your own? Explain.

2. This chapter began with a true story about a student's proposed research. Obviously, Kia believed she should be able to conduct the study. Think about her research proposal from the perspective of the faculty advisor and the college's administration.

    a. Why might the administration want to prevent Kia from completing her study? Do they have an ethical responsibility to protect her academic freedom? Why or why not?

    b. What would you do if you were Kia's faculty advisor: Would it be better to advise Kia against developing a potentially controversial study? Argue that the administration respect academic freedom and stay out of it altogether? Or, acknowledge that students are not faculty, and then claim that they do not have academic freedom at all?

3. Multiple relationships are a common factor in mentoring relationships. Think about the issues that might arise from the relationships in this scenario:

    Shawn is a psychology major with an interest in early social and cognitive development. Shawn's research mentor, Dr. Blalock, perceives him to be a highly responsible student and suspects that he is struggling financially. This gave her an idea; she had been looking for a sitter for her two young children one or two nights each week. After their recent lab meeting, Dr. Blalock asked Shawn if he would be interested in the baby sitting job. When he hesitated, Dr. Blalock inquired about his financial situation and tried to give him advice about work ethic and taking advantage of opportunities. Shawn did not appreciate that advice, especially because he already worked as much as he could without his schedule taking a toll on his schoolwork.

Can you identify the multiple relationships that may be involved in this scenario? Dr. Blalock should consider the five principles of ethical mentoring. Which of those principles is she demonstrating here? Is she violating or at risk for violating any of those principles? Address each one.

Additional Resources

American Association of University Professors

The AAUP is the primary authority on academic freedom. You can learn more at their website, https://www.aaup.org/our-programs/academic-freedom/resources-academic-freedom

APA Center on Mentoring

The American Psychological Association is the largest professional organization in psychology. In order to support future professionals, APA's Center on Mentoring provides excellent materials on how to conceptualize and practice mentoring in education and training. http://www.apa .org/education/grad/mentor-task-force.aspx

References

American Association of University Professors. (1940). *1940 statement of principles on academic freedom and tenure*. Retrieved from https://www.aaup.org/report/1940-statement-principles-academic-freedom-and-tenure

American Psychological Association. (2017). *Ethical principles of psychologists and code of conduct*. Retrieved from http://www.apa.org/ethics/code/

Anderson, D. D., & Shore, W. J. (2008). Ethical issues and concerns associated with mentoring undergraduate students. *Ethics & Behavior, 18*, 1–25.

Barnett, J. E. (2008). Mentoring, boundaries, and multiple relationships: Opportunities and challenges. *Mentoring & Tutoring: Partnership in Learning, 16*, 3–16.

Campbell, D. E., & Campbell, T. A. (2000). The mentoring relationship: Differing perceptions of benefits. *College Student Journal, 34*, 516–523.

Kuh, G. (2008). *High-impact educational practices: What they are, who has access to them, and why they matter*. Washington, DC: Association of American Colleges and Universities.

Linn, M. C., Palmer, E., Baranger, A., Gerard, E., & Stone, E. (2015). Undergraduate research experiences: Impacts and opportunities. *Science, 347*(6222).

Lopatto, D. (2006). Undergraduate research as a catalyst for liberal learning. *Peer Review, 8*, 22–25.

ETHICS OF
COLLABORATION

*Joseph and Ryan are two undergraduate psychology majors collecting
data for their senior project on the effect of race and socioeconomic status
on jurors' perceptions of witness credibility. They are required to work
in pairs to design and carry out their capstone project. Ryan becomes
increasingly frustrated with Joseph's work habits as he expects Joseph
to complete his work at the same pace and respond in a timely manner
to his emails about the project. To minimize the frustration they are both
experiencing, Joseph and Ryan choose to collect data separately and then
combine the data for the final analyses. Once Ryan collects his data, he
decides that he is not going to "share" the data with Joseph because he
does not feel that Joseph has contributed equally to the project.*

Who owns the data in this joint project? Can Ryan ethically keep his half of the data
from his collaborator? In this chapter, we will discuss ethical dilemmas that can
arise in collaborative research. Next, we will explore the guidelines for determining who
owns the data and who is allowed to present or publish the research.

ETHICAL VALUES IN
COLLABORATIVE RESEARCH

It is rare for scientists to work by themselves when conducting research. Most often, colleagues, graduate students, paid research assistants, and even undergraduates contribute

to a research project. Student researchers almost always work with peers and under the supervision of a faculty mentor. These working relationships have the potential to increase productivity and, just as important, can be very rewarding on a personal level. However, interpersonal and ethical issues can easily arise. Shamoo and Resnick (2015) identified five key values that lead to the most successful collaborations: cooperation, collegiality, trust, fairness, and accountability.

Researchers must share information and resources and coordinate efforts to attain a mutual goal. *Cooperation* requires collegial and trusting relationships. When working with others, researchers must *trust* that their collaborators will provide accurate information. This includes things like following the approved research protocol, keeping accurate records, and sharing information openly and honestly with all collaborators. *Collegiality* includes treating all members of a research team or lab with respect and dignity. When researchers collaborate, they still retain some individual incentives or rewards. These may include such things as intellectual property rights and authorship or acknowledgment on the publication of the research. Therefore, when working with other scientists, all contributing parties should be treated with *fairness* and their contributions acknowledged appropriately. Lastly, *accountability* means that all parties involved in a research project must be able to justify the work that has been done.

These five values should be considered before a project begins, and should continue after it is completed. Most completed research is documented and presented in some form, and this report may exist for years to come, particularly in peer-reviewed publications. Each individual on a research team is accountable for that final product, regardless of which tasks they completed (i.e., recruiting participants, data collection, data analysis, writing up the final paper). If mistakes were made or questionable actions were taken during the research, an individual may not be responsible for that particular action but may be held accountable for lack of oversight, review, or supervision (Shamoo & Resnick, 2015). Thus, teams that are open, collegial, and accountable work together to make sure each task is carried out correctly, accurately, and ethically.

DATA OWNERSHIP

Most students assume that if they design a study and collect the data, then they own the data. However, that is not necessarily the case. In fact, even your professor may not be able to claim ownership. When a university provides resources, such as lab space, equipment, computers, and wages, it owns the data collected in the research activities generated by faculty, staff, and students. Why does it matter who owns data? Ownership is connected to both the responsibility to maintain, share, and store data records as well as who is entitled to benefit from the data. Specifically, this determines who is able to present, publish, or share the data.

Data ownership should be established when a research project is initiated. All of the parties involved should determine this agreement: those who collected the data, those who funded the collection of data, those who have access to the data, and those responsible for storing and maintaining the data (Horner & Minifie, 2011). Although ownership technically goes to the university, most decisions regarding the use of data go to the **principal investigator** (often referred to as the PI), *the lead researcher on a study*. The PI has the unique knowledge, skills, and training to design and carry out the research. Therefore, institutions generally assign the principal investigator to be the custodian of the data. The **custodian** is *the person in charge of collecting, accessing, analyzing, storing, protecting, and maintaining the data.* The custodian also can publish the data in research papers and give presentations of the results.

Data ownership can be a complex matter at the professional level. For example, when researchers receive grants from governments or nonprofit foundations, the grant money is given to the university, not the individual researcher. In most cases, the institution owns the data, but the funding agency has the right to access the data for its own purposes. Interestingly, if a PI leaves to take a position with another university, he or she typically remains the custodian, even though ownership remains at the original institution. With students, however, ownership is usually less complicated and is often stipulated in a university-wide policy. One example of a data ownership policy for students comes from the University of New Hampshire (UNH, 2016). The policy states that UNH owns all research data generated by students in *any* of the following circumstances if the student investigator:

1. Performed the research while supported by university funds, including salary, wages, or a stipend.

2. Used facilities or equipment owned by the university for the research project.

3. Earned course credit or conducted the project for a thesis or dissertation.

What about when students graduate or leave a lab? Can they take data with them? The answer is maybe. Some institutions have stipulations granting data ownership to faculty and students, and this accounts for the fact that students are, by definition, at the university only for a very limited time. The UNH policy stipulates that when a student investigator leaves the institution, he or she may take a copy of the data but the principal investigator retains the original data.

If you are engaged in research, it is almost certain that others are involved: peer collaborators, a mentor, and perhaps your mentor's colleagues from other departments or even universities. Before beginning any research project, the responsibilities and expectations should be mapped out. It is important for students, mentors and collaborators to review the data ownership policies of their institutions as related to the presentation and publication of data. In the opening vignette, Ryan and Joseph struggled in part because they did not understand who owned the data that they collected together. Further, the research supervisor failed to discuss the issue with the students before they began collecting data. So, how was the situation resolved? In this case, the research supervisor intervened, albeit a little late, to clarify that neither of them own the data. The supervisor explained that they developed the research idea, design, experimental materials, and protocol together. Therefore, they share custody of the data. This means they are both entitled to have a copy of the data for analysis and final write-up. Because the college provided the resources to support the research, the college owns the data.

The primary goal of conducting research is to share the findings with the scientific community or public. Sharing the results of a research study takes the form of either a presentation at a conference, meeting, or a written report, journal article, or book. When researchers publish their study in a journal or book, they sign over the ownership or **copyright,** *the legal right to print and publish the research,* to a publisher. However, copyright law is limited to the written work and does not apply to data or ideas. It is not until the research is written up for publication that a copyright license is granted and then transferred to the publisher.

Not understanding who owns your data or not having an agreement with the owner of your data may interfere with sharing your research findings—a topic we turn to next.

AUTHORSHIP

Ashley has worked in her psychology professor's lab for two years on a series of experiments to determine if engaging in risk-taking behaviors increases impulsivity. She has helped conduct three experiments, including setting up the experiments in the lab, recruiting participants, and entering data. Last year, she even presented results at a psychology conference with her professor. Ashley is heading to graduate school next year to earn a PhD in behavioral neuroscience. She was surprised to find out that she would not be included as an author on the research publication. Ashley was very disappointed that her work would not be acknowledged.

Ashley's professor failed to include her in a discussion about authorship. How did her professor come to this decision? How do you determine if someone should be listed as an author?

In the academic world, authorship represents more than just having your name listed on a paper. It represents your professional productivity, status, and expertise. Faculty are often evaluated on the quality and number of publications in consideration of tenure and promotion decisions, both of which are related to job security and salary. In addition, having multiple publications often provides access to additional funding through grants and awards. Being the first author carries prestige as it signifies that you were the principal investigator and main contributor to a project. Some institutions may even require a certain number of first author publications for tenure and promotion. Being listed second or later in the list of authors does not say nearly as much about your level of contribution; you may have contributed almost as much as the PI or you may have contributed only enough to earn a spot on the author list.

Authorship goes beyond individual rewards. Authorship also comprises accountability. If your name appears on a publication as an author, you are accountable for the accuracy and truthfulness of the work in the research report. You should be able to explain and defend the methodology and results. Although not every individual on a research collaboration may contribute equally or participate in every step of the research process, each author is responsible for his or her individual contribution as well as the entire project (Shamoo & Resnick, 2015). So, who should be included as an author? Determining authorship may be more difficult than you think. Professional organizations offer authorship guidelines for publication of research. For example, the American Psychological Association's *Ethical Principles of Psychologists and Code of Conduct* (2010, Section 8.12, p. 11) includes the following criteria for authorship of a scholarly work:

1. Psychologists take responsibility and credit, including authorship credit, only for work they have actually performed or to which they have substantially contributed.

2. Principal authorship and other publication credits accurately reflect the relative scientific or professional contributions of the individuals involved, regardless

of their relative status. Mere possession of an institutional position, such as department chair, does not justify authorship credit. Minor contributions to the research or to the writing for publications are acknowledged appropriately, such as in footnotes or in an introductory statement.

3. Except under exceptional circumstances, a student is listed as principal author on any multiple-authored article that is substantially based on the student's doctoral dissertation. Faculty advisors discuss publication credit with students as early as feasible and throughout the research and publication process as appropriate.

The APA principles bring up several important concepts related to the values of collaborative research. The first relates to fairness—take credit only for work that you performed and be sure that you made a *substantial contribution* if you are to be listed as an author. The second is trust. When collaborating with other researchers, authorship expectations should be discussed from the beginning of the project, and substantial contributions should be acknowledged with authorship credit. Of course, this raises an important question: What distinguishes a substantial or professional contribution from a minor contribution? Several research studies have explored questions of authorship and authorship order. Two research activities are deemed important in the authorship debate (Wagner, Dodds, & Bundy, 1994). The first is the conceptualization or idea for the research. Many agree that if a researcher came up with the idea, research question, or design, he or she has made a substantial contribution. The second is writing the manuscript for publication. However, there are many other roles and responsibilities in carrying out a research project such as data collection, analysis, and interpretation. It is important to establish roles and responsibilities from the outset of a project so that authorship can be negotiated more easily. A recent study found that when researchers relied on guidelines to determine authorship and authorship order, authors were more satisfied with the outcome (Geelhoed, Phillips, Fischer, Shpungin, & Gong, 2007). However, a little over a quarter of those surveyed felt there was some unethical decision making with regard to authorship credit. Therefore, we recommend guidelines, author agreements, and a process for adjudicating disagreements.

Guidelines for Establishing Authorship and Authorship Order

First, you will need to negotiate authorship credit, that is, who gets to put their names on the presentation or publication. As noted in the APA principles, not everyone involved in a research project ends up as an author on the paper or presentation. For example, research assistants who help recode data or enter data into a spreadsheet may not earn authorship credit but may be acknowledged in a footnote on the first page of the journal article. Second, you will want to determine the order of authors so that each researcher can determine how much they will contribute to the final write-up of the research. Shamoo and Resnick (2015) provide fairly specific guidelines for how authorship and authorship order should be determined. They suggest that first authors should have contributed to the research idea or design, performed data analysis and interpretation, contributed most of the writing of the article, and be responsible for the final draft to be published. Further, they suggest that any coauthor must contribute in at least two of the aforementioned activities. Authorship order should reflect the relative contribution of individuals to a publication or presentation with multiple authors. Usually, the principal investigator or lead researcher's name is listed first. We must note that authorship order has some discipline-specific implications. For example, in the biomedical sciences, it is common practice for the head of the lab that produced the research to list his or her name last.

Student-Faculty Research Projects

When students collaborate with one another on a project, they may be able to more easily negotiate author order. However, it may be more complicated when students work with faculty on research. Student–faculty collaborations are inherently unequal, as professors have more power, authority, and status than their students. Fine and Kurdek (1993) identified two significant ethical issues in faculty-student collaborations: unearned authorship credit by faculty and unearned authorship credit by students. In the first case, faculty claim at least some of the authorship credit earned by the student. This can include putting their names as first author based on seniority, even when they contributed minimally, or adding their names for minimally supervising the research. It might be a student's senior research project or another project where the student is the primary investigator. At times, students may wish to include a professor's name to raise the status of the research—an ethical problem called *honorary or guest authorship*.

The second issue identified by Fine and Kurdek (1993) occurs when a student earns authorship credit without making a substantial or meaningful contribution to the research. Fine and Kurdek identified three reasons why this is an ethical problem. First, unearned authorship credit gives employers and graduate schools an expectation of competence that the student may or may not have. This impacts the student as well, potentially setting them up for failure. Finally, a student who has a publication compared to one without a publication may have an unearned advantage when applying for a job or to graduate school. Of course, this would come at the expense of other applicants who may have followed authorship guidelines more appropriately.

Disagreements and misunderstandings about what constitutes a significant or professional contribution can arise; therefore, Fine and Kurdeck (1993, p. 1145) define a professional contribution as one "that is creative and intellectual in nature, that is integral to completion of the paper, and that requires an overarching perspective of the project." A professional contribution goes beyond just looking for relevant research articles, collecting or entering data, or running research participants. Fine and Kurdeck specify that professional contributions include tasks such as contributing to the design and methodology of the research study, creating materials or assessments, making decisions about how to analyze and interpret the data, and writing sections of the manuscript. They further clarify that students and faculty should decide how many of these activities are required for authorship and that receiving payment for work on a project should not include or exclude someone from earning authorship. Research agreements and assessments, such as Winston (1985), are useful tools for determining authorship and authorship order.

In the scenario describing Ashley's experience, it appears that she contributed mostly to data collection. As Winston (1985) notes, some very important tasks involved in a research project, such as data collection, do not require significant research training or experience. According to the APA guidelines, those contributions may be appropriately acknowledged in a footnote. However, there is some indication that authors who primarily contribute to data collection are included as authors, but not first or second (Geelhoed et al., 2007). It is clear that Ashley's professor did not discuss authorship credit with her during the two years that she assisted on the project. It is possible that Ashley's professor did not believe she had the expertise to be accountable as an author on the publication. In addition, she may not have made a significant contribution to the overall project from initial conceptualization to execution and writing up the results for publication. Her professor may also have felt that giving a presentation at a conference acknowledged her role in the project and served as her reward.

In Appendix A (pp. 28–34), you will find an example of a research agreement for students working with a faculty member (Roig, 2007). The agreement includes a schedule of work to be completed as well as a quantitative evaluation of a student's contribution to a project. We are particularly fond of this agreement because it asks students to acknowledge both the professional code of ethics in the discipline as well as the institution's academic integrity policy. It also addresses data ownership and the long-term maintenance, storage, and access to the data (further addressed in Chapter 9). This form can be modified to establish agreements between student researchers as well.

Revisiting Authorship Agreements

What happens if someone fails to meet his or her obligations to a research project? This is an opportunity to revisit a research agreement and renegotiate the roles, responsibilities, and authorship credit. If there had been a research agreement between Joseph and Ryan, the research supervisor could have reviewed the roles and responsibilities and renegotiated authorship credit or order. At the end of the chapter, we have provided several resources for addressing and revisiting authorship agreements. Some take the form of checklists, and others take a quantitative approach assigning points to different research activities. We recommend choosing an approach that fits the type of research you are conducting and the level of collaboration expected.

Chapter Summary

- Cooperation, collegiality, trust, fairness, and accountability are key values in research collaboration.

- Principal investigators may serve as the custodian of research data, but ownership is determined by institutional policies.

- An individual should make a significant contribution to the research to earn authorship credit. Unearned authorship poses several ethical problems.

- In collaborative research, research agreements are useful for determining authorship and authorship order.

- Collaborators should revisit authorship credit throughout the research process.

Discussion Questions

1. Using the additional resources at the end of the chapter, how could Ashley approach her professor about her authorship concerns? Consider what questions she should ask and how her professor might answer them based on the ethical guidelines for authorship.

2. Since Ashley plans to begin a PhD program after graduation, she will likely continue a similar line of research working in her new lab. Can she take the data she collected with her? Why or why not? Under what circumstances might she be allowed to take the data with her to use in the future?

3. Does your institution have a specific data ownership policy? What about your department? If not, how might a research agreement address issues of ownership and authorship?

Additional Resources

APA's Tips for Determining Authorship Credit

The American Psychological Association (APA) offers tips and resources for negotiating authorship. It also includes a list of common reasons for changing authorship, a helpful tool for students who would like to initiate a conversation with a faculty supervisor.

http://www.apa.org/science/leadership/students/authorship-paper.aspx

Determining Authorship Order in Research Publications

In his article, Winston (1985) provides a very useful point-based method for determining authorship. This procedure is helpful for establishing authorship and authorship order as well as renegotiating throughout the research process.

Winston, R. B. (1985). A suggested procedure for determining order of authorship in research publications. *Journal of Counseling and Development, 63*, 515–518.

References

American Psychological Association. (2010). *Ethical principles of psychologists and code of conduct*. Retrieved from http://apa.org/ethics/code/index.aspx

Fine, M. A., & Kurdek, L. A. (1993). Reflections on determining authorship credit and authorship order on faculty-student collaborations. *American Psychologist, 48*, 1141–1147.

Geelhoed, R. J., Phillips, J. C., Fischer, A. R., Shpungin, E., & Gong, Y. (2007). Authorship decision making: An empirical investigation. *Ethics & Behavior, 17*, 95–115.

Horner, J., & Minifie, F. D. (2011). Research ethics II: Mentoring, collaboration, peer review, and data management and ownership. *Journal of Speech, Language, and Hearing Research, 54*, S330–S345.

Roig, M. (2007). A student-faculty research agreement. Office of Teaching Resources in Psychology. Retrieved from https://teachpsych.org/resources/Documents/otrp/resources/mr07research.pdf.

Shamoo, A., & Resnick, D. (2015). *Responsible conduct of research* (3rd ed.). New York, NY: Oxford University Press.

University System of New Hampshire. (2016). UNH policy on ownership, management, and sharing of research data. *USNH Online Policy Manual* (VIII.C.1-13). Retrieved from https://www.usnh.edu/policy/unh/viii-research-policies/c-unh-policy-ownership-management-and-sharing-research-data

Wagner, M. K., Dodds, A., & Bundy, M. B. (1994). Psychology of the scientist: LXVII. Assignment of authorship credit in psychological research. *Psychological Reports, 74*, 179–187.

Winston, R. B. (1985). A suggested procedure for determining order of authorship in research publications. *Journal of Counseling and Development, 63*, 515–518.

APPENDIX A

A Student–Faculty Research Agreement

The purpose of this document is to formalize the terms of research collabora-tions between students and their mentor for the project described below. The **Student–Faculty Research Agreement** addresses some of the specific tasks, responsibilities, and other relevant issues associated with the conduct of scientific research (e.g., research ethics, data ownership, authorship). Please read and complete this form.

Title of Proposed Study: _____

Name of Faculty Member or Project Supervisor: _____

Name of Student Investigator: _____

Names of other students involved in project (each student will complete a separate Student–Faculty Agreement): _____

1. Detailed description of research project (to be completed by the student):

    _____

    _____

    _____

    _____

    _____

    _____

    _____

    _____

    _____

    _____

2. Indicate in detail how the semester is to be divided by student tasks and by deadline dates. (e.g., first two weeks will be devoted to reading and discussing secondary sources; next three weeks will be devoted to primary source research at the library; submission of an outline in the sixth week)

    1st week _____

    2nd week _____

3rd week _____

4th week _____

5th week _____

6th week _____

7th week _____

8th week _____

9th week _____

10th week _____

11th week _____

12th week _____

13th week _____

14th week _____

Agreement Statement

I ,_____, recognize that scientific research is a labor-intensive enterprise that demands a high level of personal commitment, time, and effort. This is particularly true when the research project is being undertaken for academic credit (e.g., independent research, senior seminar) and the project must be completed within the temporal limitations of a semester-long course. By signing this document, I promise to dedicate the necessary time and effort to complete this project in accordance to the schedule drawn above. I will also uphold the principles of scientific integrity as exemplified by the APA Ethics Code http://www.apa.org/ethics/code/index.aspx, particularly Principle C and Standard 8, Research & Publication, which I have read and understood. I have also reviewed our institution's academic integrity policies, and I am fully aware of the seriousness of these issues and of the consequences of violating such policies. Based on the APA ethical principles and our own institution's academic integrity policies, I recognize that any form of data falsification, data fabrication, or plagiarism in the conduct of research is not only an academically dishonest act, but also a most severe form of scientific misconduct.

If this research project involves the recruitment and testing of human subjects, I agree to take a tutorial on the protection of human subjects (as determined by our university) before commencing work on the project.

Similarly, if the project involves using animals as subjects, I agree to complete a tutorial on the use of animals as research subjects (e.g., http://grants.nih.gov/grants/olaw/tutorial/).

I shall also abide by the stipulation that all research data (e.g., questionnaires, data files, records, observations) from this project become the property of the institution and will be retained by the faculty member who will determine who and under what circumstances others may have access to such data. I also understand that authorship of any resulting conference presentation or journal article will depend on the extent of my contributions to this project as stipulated in Standard 8.12 of the APA Ethics Code.

Student's signature _____ date _____

Faculty member's or supervising investigator's
signature _____ date _____

Chairperson's signature _____ date _____

Project Grade and Authorship Determination Rating Guide

Extent of Student Contribution to the
Project (to be completed by faculty mentor)

Please circle the item that best describes the extent to which each of the following statements describes the student's performance in the project. Leave blank if not applicable.

Introduction

- Conceptualized the study/origin of idea/hypothesis/variables

1	2	3	4	5
Not at all	To a little extent	To a moderate extent	To a great extent	To a very great extent

Method

- Carried out the literature search (identified relevant literature, retrieved articles, summarized articles)

1	2	3	4	5
Not at all	To a little extent	To a moderate extent	To a great extent	To a very great extent

- Made contributions to the research design

1	2	3	4	5
Not at all	To a little extent	To a moderate extent	To a great extent	To a very great extent

- Constructed stimulus materials/Set up-calibrated study equipment/ Carried out ratings

1	2	3	4	5
Not at all	To a little extent	To a moderate extent	To a great extent	To a very great extent

Data collection

- Recruited and consented subjects

1	2	3	4	5
Not at all	To a little extent	To a moderate extent	To a great extent	To a very great extent

- Ran subjects/Recorded observations

1	2	3	4	5
Not at all	To a little extent	To a moderate extent	To a great extent	To a very great extent

- Debriefed subjects

1	2	3	4	5
Not at all	To a little extent	To a moderate extent	To a great extent	To a very great extent

Data analyses

- Entered data in database

1	2	3	4	5
Not at all	To a little extent	To a moderate extent	To a great extent	To a very great extent

- Checked data for accuracy

1	2	3	4	5
Not at all	To a little extent	To a moderate extent	To a great extent	To a very great extent

- Contributed to data analysis decisions

1	2	3	4	5
Not at all	To a little extent	To a moderate extent	To a great extent	To a very great extent

- Carried out data analyses

1	2	3	4	5
Not at all	To a little extent	To a moderate extent	To a great extent	To a very great extent

Writing

- Wrote Introduction and literature review

1	2	3	4	5
Not at all	To a little extent	To a moderate extent	To a great extent	To a very great extent

- Wrote Methods section

1	2	3	4	5
Not at all	To a little extent	To a moderate extent	To a great extent	To a very great extent

- Wrote Results section

1	2	3	4	5
Not at all	To a little extent	To a moderate extent	To a great extent	To a very great extent

- Wrote Discussion section

1	2	3	4	5
Not at all	To a little extent	To a moderate extent	To a great extent	To a very great extent

Presentation

- Constructed poster

1	2	3	4	5
Not at all	To a little extent	To a moderate extent	To a great extent	To a very great extent

- Made presentation

1	2	3	4	5
Not at all	To a little extent	To a moderate extent	To a great extent	To a very great extent

Other contributions

- Identified potential confounds

1	2	3	4	5
Not at all	To a little extent	To a moderate extent	To a great extent	To a very great extent

- Identified possible directions for future research

1	2	3	4	5
Not at all	To a little extent	To a moderate extent	To a great extent	To a very great extent

- Organizational skills

1	2	3	4	5
Very Poor	Poor	Fair	Good	Very Good

- Dedication to the project

1	2	3	4	5
Very Poor	Poor	Fair	Good	Very Good

- Other 1: _____

  1   2   3   4   5

  _____   _____   _____   _____   _____

- Other 2: _____

  1   2   3   4   5

  _____   _____   _____   _____   _____

Additional Notes

_____

_____

_____

_____

_____

4

MANAGING RISKS WITH
HUMAN SUBJECTS

*Students in Dr. Wu's social psychology lab course were asked
to design and conduct a self-report study on one of the topics
covered in class. Fascinated by the readings on romantic and sexual
relationships, one group decided to test whether membership in
extracurricular organizations might be associated with infidelity.
The student researchers surveyed students at their small,
residential college to see if membership in groups that emphasized
stereotypical masculinity, such as the football team and fraternities,
was associated with more infidelity. While analyzing the data, Dr.
Wu overheard a student laugh and turned to see her pointing at one
participant's responses. "There's only one student who plays baseball
and is in the Delta Omega Nu fraternity—you know
who that is, right? Check out what he wrote!" Dr. Wu was alarmed,
and told the students to delete their data immediately because they
had broken their promise of anonymity.*

The majority of research in psychology involves the cooperation of people who are
referred to as *participants* in APA style. The general term used in most scientific
discourse is **human subject**, which is defined as *a living individual from whom a
researcher obtains (1) data through intervention or interaction with the individual or
(2) identifiable private information*. The safety and well-being of human subjects may

be the most thoroughly established and discussed form of research ethics. It is taught in almost all methods courses in the social sciences and other disciplines that involve studying humans. Although these principles are foremost designed to avoid severe, possibly even fatal illness or injury, you will see that psychological research involves several other forms of risk, each of which should be assessed at multiple stages of the research process. Consideration of potential risk to participants should begin before seeking approval for a research study. As you think of the various ways to test a hypothesis, you need to be aware of the risks associated with different approaches. Before we get into the specifics of protecting human subjects, let's look back in history to the origins of human protections in research.

HUMAN SUBJECTS PROTECTIONS

We take many ethical principles in research for granted today, as if it is obvious how we should treat human subjects. However, if you look back at the 20th century, you will find numerous examples of research activities that are so clearly unethical by today's standards that it is shocking. One well-known example is the Tuskegee Syphilis Study, which took place in southern Alabama beginning in the 1930's. In this study, several hundred Black men who had syphilis were told they would receive treatment if they participated in longitudinal research on "bad blood." However, these men did not receive treatment, even after effective drugs became widely available (Cave & Holm, 2003; Thomas & Quinn, 1991). Outright racism and prejudice against lower socioeconomic status groups allowed the researchers to essentially watch these men suffer and die. Although contemporary volunteers go untreated in placebo conditions, consider the lack of education and job opportunities available to African Americans in that place and time. Without additional information about the study, how could the Tuskegee men be expected to ask whether there would be a placebo condition, or what their chances were of not being treated? Even if they had known, consider the scarce resources and options for medical care they must have faced. Would they really have any other choices for possible medical treatment? In fact, the researchers lied to the men about the study and did not inform them of the available treatment.

The Tuskegee Syphilis Study continued largely unknown to outsiders until the early 1970's when word of the human rights abuses became public. In response, the U.S. government established the National Research Act in 1974. Many governments have enacted similar protections that are enforced with legal and civil penalties. In addition nongovernmental organizations, such as the World Health Organization, and professional groups, such as the American Psychological Association and the Society for Neuroscience, that support or rely on scientific research have policies and regulations in place to prevent such abuses.

The National Research Act of 1974 established the current set of protections for human subjects in the United States. The U.S. Department of Health and Human Services oversees the rules and regulations of the ethical treatment of human subjects in their **Office of Human Research Protections (OHRP)**. (Although the standards are different, organizations have developed ethical codes for the treatment of animal subjects as well—these will be addressed in Chapter 6.) Unfortunately, researchers still violate these protections on occasion, which is particularly worrisome when dealing with vulnerable populations, such as children, pregnant women, and those with mental or cognitive disabilities. In these cases, the OHRP takes on the role of enforcing federal guidelines and may seek criminal charges or sanctions in response to violations. In fact, a more recent example is the Baltimore Lead Study, which is summarized in the Discussion Questions section at the end of this chapter.

IDENTIFYING RISKS

Researchers must be diligent in identifying potential risks while designing their study, and then reduce the chance of those risks occurring during the research. Researchers want to avoid a potential risk becoming an **adverse event**: *any harm to physical, social, or psychological well-being, or any liability to a human subject as a direct result of participating in the study.* To support scientists in this process, universities require that any proposed research be approved by an independent panel. A research review committee, usually an IRB (Institutional Review Board), approves and monitors research activities involving human participants to ensure they are treated ethically. In this chapter, we will discuss the types of risk that research volunteers could face and how researchers can minimize or justify the risks. After learning about risks in this chapter, we will address the functions and procedures associated with IRBs in Chapter 5.

Assessing, Reducing, and Justifying Risks

In an ideal world, research participants would not face the possibility of harm, but for many topics of research, there is some risk involved. In fact, there are four main categories of risk that researchers should consider as they design their studies:

- *Risk of physical harm.* Could participation result in any temporary discomfort, any type of injury, or increase the risk of illness?

- *Risk of social harm.* Could participation cause damage to one's reputation, disrupt individual relationships, limit participation in groups, or even cost someone a job?

- *Risk of psychological harm.* Does the research involve any psychological stressors or exposure to unpleasant or offensive stimuli? These would be considered risky if they are likely to cause significant or long-lasting discomfort or distress.

- *Risk of punishment or liability.* Does participation involve violating campus policies, breaking the law, or putting oneself at risk for a civil lawsuit? Are participants being asked to admit to prior behaviors that produce the same types of risk?

Some forms of risk are not so obvious. Consider the student who wanted to investigate the effect of sleep deprivation on accuracy of shooting basketballs. The experiment was well-designed but happened to be planned for the week before final exams. The impact of purposely depriving students of sleep (more so than normal, of course) right before final exams might be considered harmful given the consequences of performing badly on a final exam. What type of risk might this be? Is it enough to tell participants ahead of time what you are asking them to do? Can they make an informed decision in their own best interest? What if you are offering an incentive that they really want? All of these questions should be addressed as you develop your methods and make plans for data collection. Because there are four main categories of risk, a researcher will likely need to find more than one method of reducing the overall risk involved in participation. In some cases, one method can be used to prevent multiple types of adverse events. For example, ensuring anonymity and confidentiality goes a long way toward preventing adverse social or legal consequences. But in many other cases, multiple steps will need to be taken in order to control all the risks present in a research design. We will start with perhaps the most powerful means of prevention once the research design is complete: giving potential volunteers the knowledge and choice to assess their own tolerance for risk.

Informed Consent and Right to Withdraw

One of the foundations of human research protections is **informed consent:** *a formal acknowledgment from prospective human subjects that (1) they are aware of and understand any risks and benefits associated with participation, and (2) they are willing to accept those conditions and to begin the study.* This is a multifaceted definition, but at a very basic level, informed consent is exactly what it sounds like: For human subjects to be informed, the researcher must explain what the purpose of the study is and what their participation involves, including potential risks and benefits. For human subjects to give consent, they must be able to exercise a knowledgeable choice without feeling pressured to do so. It is important, however, that anyone designing and conducting a study go beyond just a basic understanding of informed consent. This is because verbally agreeing to something is not necessarily a free choice. There are many subtle ways in which participants can feel pressured to begin or continue a study despite their wishes not to. Similarly, just knowing about the study is not the same as knowing what it entails. There are certainly examples, such as the Tuskegee study, where participants did not know that researchers sometimes withhold treatment. It is also important for the researchers to know how much to explain in advance; many psychological studies require that the participants do not know exactly what they are getting into. Obviously, that poses a threat to the "informed" aspect of informed consent.

Federal regulations state that before volunteers participate in a study, the researcher must provide the following to fully obtain informed consent. These are the exact regulations from the Department of Health and Human Services, Section 46.116 (2009, pp. 16–17):

1) A statement that the study involves research, an explanation of the purposes of the research and the expected duration of the subject's participation, a description of the procedures to be followed, and identification of any procedures which are experimental;

2) A description of any reasonably foreseeable risks or discomforts to the subject;

3) A description of any benefits to the subject or to others which may reasonably be expected from the research;

4) A disclosure of appropriate alternative procedures or courses of treatment, if any, that might be advantageous to the subject;

5) A statement describing the extent, if any, to which confidentiality of records identifying the subject will be maintained;

6) For research involving more than minimal risk, an explanation as to whether any compensation and any medical treatments are available if injury occurs and, if so, what they consist of or where further information may be obtained;

7) An explanation of whom to contact for answers to pertinent questions about the research and research subjects' rights, and whom to contact in the event of a research-related injury to the subject; and

8) A statement that participation is voluntary, refusal to participate will involve no penalty or loss of benefits to which the subject is otherwise entitled, and the subject may discontinue participation at any time without penalty or loss of benefits to which the subject is otherwise entitled.

An important note about informed consent is that only legal, capable adults can give informed consent. Therefore, anyone under the age of 18 cannot give informed consent to participate in a study. Researchers conducting studies with children or adolescents must obtain informed consent from a parent or legal guardian. Typically, researchers also seek **assent:** *permission to participate in research by someone who is legally unable to give informed consent.* Assent is not legally binding, but it does assure researchers that the participants willingly participated. Although the regulations for consent are very clear, we sometimes forget that there are college students under the age of 18. In one case we are aware of, two graduate students at a large university went into an undergraduate class and collected data using anonymous surveys. It was later determined that two students enrolled in the class and who participated in the research were under 18, and the IRB was informed of the incident. Because the surveys were anonymous, there was no way to determine which surveys belonged to the underage students. Therefore, the IRB decided that the researchers had violated a fundamental, ethical principle and instructed them to throw out all of the data they had collected. This was, of course, a devastating blow to the researchers and a hard way to learn about research ethics. But, it does bring us to our next topic: anonymity and confidentiality.

Providing for Confidentiality and Anonymity

From an ethical viewpoint, anonymity and confidentiality are meant to protect individual participants in case their responses could damage their reputations or get them into trouble. Confidentiality of participants is always a requirement of human subjects research. In fact, confidentiality also extends to those who choose not to participate; it is possible that declining to participate can have the same negative consequences as participating. It is important to include a mechanism that allows individuals to both accept or decline the invitation without risk of retaliation. There are a variety of solutions to these problems, depending on your research methods. One strategy is to use an electronic sign-up sheet or website for online experiments and self-report studies; there are many online services that allow this so you should check to see what is available on your campus. As a researcher, you should not discuss or disclose to others who participated in your study. You may, however, share the names of participants (not the data) to the person providing the incentive (e.g., a professor giving extra credit).

If collecting data in person, anonymity can be preserved by having individuals respond on paper in a location or manner that prevents the researchers from seeing the responses. At the end of data collection, paper forms can be submitted into a locked box that remains unopened until all data are collected. This is effective as long as the submitted responses are not in order when retrieved from the box. Many researchers are turning to online data collection techniques to conduct research, often relying on web-based survey software, such as Survey Monkey or Qualtrics. While these can make data collection easy and fast, it is important to make sure you are not inadvertently collecting personal information such as IP addresses, which identify the geographic location of a respondent. Make sure that these software options are turned off or that they do not reveal an individual's identity. There are additional risks related to online data collection techniques. These are explored more in the additional resources at the end of the chapter.

From a purely methodological viewpoint, research participants are often more honest and candid when they know their responses are anonymous—that was probably the case for participants in the example that opened this chapter. Some research involves the study of **sensitive topics:** *subject matters that increase social risks and risks for legal problems or liability.* Sensitive topics include anything that people might want to conceal or protect, such as their criminal records, physical or mental health conditions and treatment, illicit drug use, sexual behavior, or even grades. When studying a sensitive topic, it is a good idea to provide for anonymity when possible. This may seem easier to do online, but it is certainly possible to collect data in person and maintain anonymity of responses. For example, we know of more than one study that linked types of personal information, such as substance use or criminal record, with behavioral data or physiological responses to certain stimuli. The researchers in both of these cases needed to be present to collect physiological data, so they were challenged to link the data they directly observed with anonymously collected self-report data. Can you think of a way to maintain anonymity in those situations? Here is one example of a research protocol used by a student and research supervisor to protect sensitive, personal information:

Electrodermal responses will be recorded by a computer with the researcher present to operate the equipment and software. Each participant's recording will be stored along with the participant's unique number so it will not be identified by name. Next, the participant will complete the self-report portion of the study, which will begin with the participant recording her or his unique number. In order to maintain the anonymity of the self-report information, the researcher will not have access to these data until later. Following all the data collection, the self-report data will be downloaded by the faculty supervisor, who will then match those data to the physiological recordings in a single spreadsheet. After deleting the participant ID numbers, he will share it with the researcher. This way, neither the researcher nor the advisor will be able to identify the participants corresponding to any one piece of data.

As you can see, maintaining confidentiality and anonymity can require careful planning and additional work. However, it is clearly worth it both for the ethical concerns and the quality of the data.

BENEFITS OF RESEARCH

If so many ethical principles are about minimizing risk, why should we tolerate risk at all? A simple answer is that very few things in life are risk-free. You may reduce risk by wearing a seatbelt and following traffic regulations when driving. However, driving is fundamentally risky, and the only way to eliminate the risk completely is to stay inside as far away from traffic as possible. Driving a car affords us many opportunities like independence and autonomy and assists in maintaining personal and professional relationships. Just like the risks involved with driving, the benefits of facing those risks are sometimes greater than the hazards. It is up to the researcher to identify the risks and the benefits, then to weigh them against each other: Does the potential benefit outweigh the potential harm?

Earlier, we identified four categories of risk, but there are probably only two categories of benefits: personal and scientific. Personal benefits can be as mundane as a few points of extra credit or something monumental such as the potential for free treatment of a life-threatening illness. For student researchers, personal benefits may range from completing an honors program, to gaining a master's degree, or even maintaining a full-time job as a research assistant.

More often than not, researchers should emphasize the scientific benefits of their work. These, too, can vary widely. We would argue that student-run projects have the benefits of training future scientists and developing scientific literacy, among others. For the professional researcher, studies can have several types of benefits:

- *Theoretical*: Contributing to understanding and explaining a phenomenon.

- *Clinical*: Contributing to the prevention and treatment of medical or psychological problems.

- *Practical*: Solving real-world problems.

Regardless of the types of risks, there may be benefits that can be used to justify the research—addressing this is an important part of designing a research study. Consider some of the risks and benefits we have touched on so far. Imagine putting them on a balance opposite each other and ask which is greater? The risk or the benefit? Consider a high-risk study, such as one in which participants will be exposed to potential painful stimuli. Is there ever a time when such risk is justifiable? Weigh that risk against these potential benefits:

- A volunteer will receive three points of extra credit on a 100-point exam.

- An undergraduate will complete an honors project.

- A graduate student has a chance of finding something useful in her study.

- A medical researcher is working toward developing a novel treatment for fibromyalgia.

If you are like most people, three points of extra credit or helping a student complete an honors project are not worth the possibility of severe pain; these are personal benefits that can probably be achieved in other ways. But, what about the professional who has a high likelihood of developing a treatment for debilitating, lifelong pain? You might be able to argue that the clinical benefit outweighs the physical risk. If the researcher can ensure that potential volunteers know exactly what chance they have for an adverse event, and how severe and long-lasting the pain might be, then they can make their own decision about whether to consent to the study.

Occasionally, researchers will use **deception**: *withholding specific information about a research study or experiment that could influence participants' behavior or the outcome of the study.* For example, a stress manipulation often used in research is to tell participants that they will have to give a speech on a topic they know little about, and they have 10 minutes to prepare. In one such study, participants were led to believe that a group of faculty were evaluating them behind a one-way mirror. Participants' stress response was measured at the end of the speech by collecting saliva and testing for cortisol levels. Sometimes, deception is necessary to be able to study real human behaviors or reactions. Deception is an acceptable practice when it is used appropriately and when the benefits of deception outweigh the potential risks. Most importantly, a researcher cannot withhold information about risk in a consent form. What that means is, you cannot lie about the potential risks in a study. Secondly, if deception is used, then researchers must debrief participants when participation ends or when the study is completed. **Debriefing** *is telling the participants the truth about the experiment after it is completed and making sure that they are in the same physical, mental, or emotional state they were in when they arrived for the study.*

CHALLENGES UNIQUE TO STUDENT RESEARCHERS

Student researchers will almost always approach their own research under a different set of circumstances than the professional researchers for whom ethical principles were designed. In this last section, we address some of these unique challenges and apply the PASA model to help students and their research mentors identify and weigh the risks and benefits associated with a research study. In Table 4.1, we explore how student researchers compare to professionals.

A Note About Student Researchers

We both teach at small, liberal arts colleges. There are times when a topic being studied is more challenging at a small school where many students know each other. For example, during experimental manipulations it is often difficult to have people you know participate in a study; this can affect both the researcher and subject. The stress study mentioned earlier was a student-run experiment. Participants were told that a speech they had to prepare was being judged by professors who were observing through a one-way mirror. Because students know their professors pretty well at a smaller school, the stress experienced by some of the participants was particularly intense. In addition, it was difficult for the student researchers to watch a peer experience that level of stress response while "acting" like a researcher. In another study, a student designed an experiment to see if college students would cheat on a task to gain a reward. Although it was well-designed to maintain anonymous responses

TABLE 4.1 ■ Unique Characteristics of Student Research	
Compared to Professionals, Student Researchers . . .	**Potential Consequences**
have less background knowledge	The study is less likely to produce scientific benefits
have less experience and skill	Inexperience increases risk of adverse events due to errors
usually have a limited pool of potential volunteers	Small populations increase difficulty in protecting anonymity and confidentiality, thereby increasing social and liability risks
are more likely to have contact with participants outside of the research context	Personal relationships may increase pressure for consent. They also make anonymity and confidentiality more difficult to achieve
have no professional qualifications	Untrained individuals may not recognize when or know how to respond appropriately if adverse events occur

(participants threw away their self-scored matrix problems), the student researcher was known on campus and had to hire an outside person to serve as the experimenter. Although she was not present during the experiment itself participants saw her name on the informed consent form. Interestingly, no one cheated! We have to believe that the lack of cheating was influenced by the small community in which the research was conducted. Another possibility was that participants knew the researcher and were careful not to cheat. The student had to secure additional research sites to collect data for her study to ensure that she was not inadvertently influencing the results of her experiment. Lastly, although they may be very interested, undergraduate students may not be prepared to study some sensitive topics. What if someone discloses depression or suicidal ideation? How does a student researcher handle that information? What is the responsibility of the student and the research advisor? These are important questions to explore before designing a student-led study.

Recruiting Participants

Because student researchers have limited access to human subjects, they are often tempted to recruit their friends to participate in their research projects. At first, this may seem harmless, but it presents both ethical and methodological problems. When you recruit someone you know face-to-face or in front of others, they may feel pressured to agree to participate, especially when there are what the APA calls *multiple relationships* (a concept introduced in Chapter 2). A senior conducting a research project may also be an officer in a sorority or captain of a sports team. When recruiting a younger student, that researcher is also a person in power, and that dual relationship makes it more difficult for the younger student to say no. This illustrates an important ethical issue to address, not to mention the methodological problem of a very limited, homogenous sample.

As research mentors, we advise our students to approach recruitment in a systematic manner that aims to reach larger groups of potential participants without singling out individuals or small groups. This can be accomplished through postings on a campus portal, putting notices up in public areas, making announcements in classes or group meetings, and even emailing out to large groups on campus. Of course there are times when you need specific groups of students, such as musicians; it is fine to target specific groups, again as long as there are mechanisms—such as anonymity—to reduce any pressure to participate.

APPLYING THE PASA MODEL

Let's consider how some of these differences might emerge during a student's research and what students might do to address them.

Principles: The ethical principles in this chapter are based largely on the values of beneficence and nonmaleficence. Anonymity and confidentiality protect human subjects from social, legal, and liability risks. Informed consent informs participants of the risks and benefits of the research.

Assumptions: These principles assume that research is conducted by professionals who have training in research ethics and have a greater chance of producing meaningful scientific benefits.

Status: When comparing students to professionals, we are likely to find more personal benefits (especially educational) than scientific. Additionally, student researchers do not have the knowledge, skill, or resources as a professional, which affects the potential for benefits and risk. Review the types of risks and benefits we covered in this chapter, and you will likely find that student research differs from professional in several ways, as shown in Table 4.1.

Adaptation: Based on the status differences, we should place greater emphasis on reducing the risks—it would be more challenging to increase benefits.

Now, let's see how we might apply this model to a real example:

An undergraduate was taking a culture and health course from a visiting professor when she became interested in self-injury. She proposed a study to the IRB that entailed sending out an anonymous survey to college students asking if they engaged in self-injuring behaviors, such as cutting oneself with sharp objects. The student wanted to know how prevalent the behavior was and which behaviors are most common among college students. She proposed the study because she was interested in learning more about the topic, not as part of a course or major requirement. In fact, her major was history.

As you go through the principles, assumptions, status of the researcher, and adaptation of the study, where do you see differences between a professional and student researcher? What additional information would you need to apply the model or decide whether or not the student should conduct the research?

Like the other examples in this book, this story actually occurred. In this particular case, the IRB spent a long time discussing the proposal and even brought in a counselor to discuss the potential risks to research participants. In the end, the IRB did not approve the study because the student did not have enough research or clinical training or appropriate supervision by a full-time faculty member. In addition, the IRB speculated that receiving a survey like this could trigger unwanted behaviors among those who engage in self-injury. In this instance, the benefits did not outweigh the risks and even put the student researcher and institution at risk, given that the information would have been anonymous. To be clear, it is not unethical to study sensitive topics like self-harm. In fact, some researchers exclusively study sensitive topics, such as sexual trauma and childhood abuse. Recently, a group of researchers found that college women with an abuse history did report distress when participating in a study on their abuse experiences but also found it to be beneficial in terms of learning about themselves and potentially helping others (Decker, Naugle, Visscher, Bell, & Seifert, 2011). The key is that the risk or potential risk to participants should not outweigh the benefits of the study and measures should be taken to protect the safety and well-being of those involved. Additional training or supervision may be necessary when studying sensitive topics.

Chapter Summary

- The need for established regulations on ethical treatment of participants arose from the poor treatment of research subjects in the past.

- Researchers should ensure the safety and well-being of human subjects who participate in psychological research before beginning the research process.

- In most cases, research that involves human participants must be approved by a review committee to ensure that any risk is justified by the benefits of the research.

- The four categories of risk are risk of physical harm, risk of social harm, risk of psychological harm, and risk of punishment or liability.

- Anonymity and confidentiality help protect individual participants by ensuring that their responses are not linked to them, especially when studying sensitive topics.

- Student researchers face a unique set of challenges due to their inexperience and newness to research. The PASA model can assist students in determining the risks and benefits of their study.

Discussion Questions

1. Once in an end-of-course evaluation, a student reported that her professor did not enroll her 3-year-old son in the student's senior research project conducted at the university's preschool. Of course, the professor may have had legitimate reasons for not doing so. However, course evaluations are read by the dean and other faculty as part of a professor's review for tenure and promotion. Based on your understanding of confidentiality, was it unethical for the student to write that in a course evaluation? Why or why not?

2. An undergraduate student wants to study trauma among college students. She is particularly interested in experiences of sexual trauma. If you were the faculty mentor or supervisor, what concerns might you have? How would you go about weighing the risks and benefits of the study?

3. In the 1990s, researchers from Johns Hopkin's Kennedy Krieger Institute (KKI) conducted a study in inner-city Baltimore on the health effects of lead paint in children. Although lead paint was banned in the United States in 1978 due to its toxic neurological effects, lead paint remains in older residences and still poses a threat, especially to children. Researchers in the Baltimore Lead Study were comparing how effective some lower cost methods of eliminating lead (e.g., lead abatement) might be at reducing lead exposure to children. They were using cheaper techniques

that only partially removed the lead. Researchers knowingly recruited low-income families, primarily African Americans, with children to live in residences that had known levels of lead in them. They tested the children's blood levels for lead over a period of years. A class action lawsuit was filed against KKI by several mothers whose children showed cognitive deficits from lead exposure and who felt that they were not completely informed of the long-term risks of the study to their children.

a. What kind of information should be disclosed in an informed consent for this study?

b. Do you think the benefits of the study justified the risks to the children?

c. If you were reviewing this research for approval, what questions would you have for the researchers?

Additional Resources

Psychological Research Online: Opportunities and Challenges

The American Psychological Association (APA) summarizes the benefits and risks of collecting data online and applies the standard ethical guidelines to conducting online research. The report addresses how online research differs from face-to-face data collection procedures and provides guidelines to protect human participants.

http://www.apa.org/science/leadership/bsa/internet/internet-report.aspx

Research With Diverse Populations

This brief report outlines ethical challenges in conducting mental health research with the ethnic-minority youth. Ethical dilemmas include how conceptions of privacy, benefits and risks of research, reliability and validity of measures, and payment for research participation may differ based on culture and socioeconomic status.

http://www.apa.org/monitor/oct01/weighissues.aspx

References

Cave, E., & Holm, S. (2003). Milgram and Tuskegee—Paradigm research projects in bioethics. *Health Care Analysis, 1*(11), 27–40.

Decker, S., Naugle, A., Visscher, R., Bell, K., & Seifert, A. (2011). Ethical issues in research on sensitive topics: Participants' experiences of distress and benefit. *Journal of Empirical Research on Human Research Ethics, 6,* 55–64.

Thomas, S. B., & Quinn, S. C. (1991). The Tuskegee syphilis study, 1932 to 1972: Implications for HIV education and AIDS risk education programs in the black community. *American Journal of Public Health, 81,* 1498–1505.

U.S. Department of Health and Human Services. (2009). 45 CFR 46, Code of Federal Regulations. Retrieved from https://www.hhs.gov/ohrp/regulations-and-policy/regulations/45-cfr-46/index.html#46.116

5

NAVIGATING THE IRB PROCESS

Allen's university held a student scholarship day in which students are invited to make poster presentations of their most significant research or creative projects. He presented quantitative data from self-report scales on substance abuse and unemployment or underemployment. To illustrate patterns in the data, he also provided quotes from his interviews with men who were living in halfway-houses after being released from high-security prison. When Allen was presenting his work, he mentioned interviewing these men at the specific address of the residence, in some cases revealing personal details such as hometown, age, and name. He also said that he had been told not to use his own name when meeting these men because, as a friend put it, "They're career criminals." A sociology professor he knew from an earlier course was interested in this study, but very quickly became concerned about the personal details Allen included from his interviews and even more so when he realized that they could not even contact Allen if they had follow-up questions about their participation in his research. The professor asked if the IRB had approved this method. It turns out Allen had not received approval from the IRB; in fact, he did not even know what "IRB" meant. At that point, an associate dean insisted that Allen take down his poster, and he was reprimanded for violating the university's ethical standards for researchers.

W hat is wrong with Allen's approach to his interviews? Why did he need to tell the men he interviewed who he was and what he was doing? What should his faculty mentor have done to help Allen follow ethical guidelines while collecting data for his project? This unfortunate event served as a reminder to the faculty and administrators involved: Students do not come to college knowing about research ethics and the steps the university takes to promote them. In this chapter, we will explore the rules and procedures used to protect human participants involved in research. Specifically, we will describe the research review process and the work of an Institutional Review Board.

INTRODUCING THE IRB

As part of their regulations, the OHRP defines the **Institutional Review Board (IRB)** as *a committee designated to approve and monitor research activities that include human participants in order to ensure they are treated ethically.* In this capacity, the committee focuses on the ethics related to the prevention of unnecessary harm, promoting justice (ensuring that all individuals are treated equally, regardless of demographic characteristics), and obtaining informed consent to participate—something that was denied the men in the Tuskegee study. Because of the importance of these protections, the OHRP maintains a permanent website where anyone may look up the regulations and find advice for how to interpret and apply them (https://www.hhs.gov/ohrp/).

Although defined at the federal level, IRBs are *institutional,* meaning that any given institution, such as a college or university, research hospital, or other organization that receives federal funding must establish its own IRB and register it with the OHRP. The regulations also specify the requirements for the types of individuals who serve on the committee. At the minimum, the institution must select a minimum of five individuals while ensuring the following types of members serve on the IRB:

- A professional who is trained and engaged in scientific research

- An individual at the institution whose specialization is in a nonscientific area

- An individual representing the human subjects' perspective (e.g., an individual with significant experience conducting or participating in human subjects research)

- An individual who is not directly affiliated with the institution

- Both men and women

In addition, institutions should ensure the members are representative of the community's diversity, which often means adding a sixth or seventh member. Also, when necessary, IRBs may seek advice from experts in a specific field who are not personally involved in the proposed research; however, these individuals are not considered IRB members and do not vote for or against approval (Department of Health and Human Services, 2009).

DEFINING RESEARCH

How Do I Know if My Project Needs IRB Approval?

The IRB rules require that all faculty and staff conducting human subjects research at your institution will need to obtain IRB approval first. This has always been applied to graduate students as well. However, undergraduate-led research has only become commonplace in the past 20 years, and it has not always been clear whether the guidelines apply to students (Kallgren & Tauber, 1996). The majority consensus finally emerged that IRB regulations apply to all research in the exact same ways.

If a researcher fails to get approval before the first piece of data is collected, then there may be serious consequences. Typically, this means that you would be required to surrender your data to the institution, and subsequently, you would not be allowed to present or publish your data. This is what happened in the scenario presented at the beginning of the chapter. Allen did not obtain informed consent from his research participants, and therefore, he could not present the data from the interviews. Other consequences for undergraduates depend on the context; it might lead to failure in a lab course and it may be treated the same as plagiarism (e.g., referral to an honor council or other presiding body). For graduate students who are expected to be more advanced, failure to obtain IRB approval is likely to lead to expulsion. There are unofficial consequences as well: If research is conducted without an advisor's support, faculty will be wary about offering additional opportunities to you or writing strong letters of recommendation. Obviously, you do not want to find yourself in that position, so it is important that you can identify what types of activities do require approval versus those that do not.

What Is Research?

This may seem like a simple question at first, but there are a few gray areas. It is important to consider the official definition of research and then compare activities that do versus do not require IRB approval. According to the OHRP guidelines, **research** is *"a systematic investigation . . . designed to develop or contribute to generalizable knowledge."* Before you begin any activity in which you gather data from or about individuals, you should check it against this definition. Have you developed a method based on scientific principles to gather information—perhaps a survey or an experiment? If so, you are doing a systematic investigation. Does this method test a hypothesis? Or, could the information gathered from it conceivably be presented at a conference or published in a journal? If so, then it is best to assume that it can contribute to generalizable knowledge and is thereby considered research, even if you are not sure that the results will be informative or interesting enough for presenting or publishing. Although there are sometimes questions about whether a project for a lab course needs IRB approval, for ethical considerations, it is often best to err on the safe side. If you are unsure, contact the chair of your institution's IRB; let that individual's opinion be the deciding factor. In Allen's case, his advisor and IRB chair would most likely have asked the following questions:

- What is your goal for this project: (a) Are you simply conducting an interview for a class? Or (b) are you trying to analyze trends or find systematic biases that help explain possible links between substance abuse and employment?

- What are you going to do with your results and conclusions: (a) Are you going to keep the results in class as a paper or classroom presentation? Or (b) do you plan to share your findings at a conference or in an academic publication?

If Allen had answered (b) for both questions, then the IRB's chairperson would likely have requested at least a brief review. Another approach would be to use the OHRP decision charts, which are available online (https://www.hhs.gov/ohrp/regulations-and-policy/decision-charts/index.html). These are very useful in decision making related to types of research and the IRB requirements for consent and approval.

What Is Exempt From Review?

Another means of deciding whether you need IRB approval is to look at the specific activities that are considered "exempt" from review. The DHHS lists a number of activities that might meet the definition of research, somewhat or in part, but do not constitute any additional risk to participants beyond their normal daily activities. For example, a teacher can collect data on student performance as part of regular class meetings, class projects, or even on homework. These data may be used to evaluate and compare the effectiveness of teaching methods and assignments. The teacher's activities are classified as exempt because they are considered "normal educational practices." In other words, students may very well be assigned the same tasks, even if the teacher was not interested in evaluating the projects or papers.

In general, research and other similar activities are considered exempt if they protect the identity and safety of the individuals and involve:

- Normal educational practices

- Observation of public behavior

- The use of archival data

- Evaluations of programs available to the public

- Consumer product studies, such as taste tests, so long as there is no question about the safety of the product

To understand these exemptions, it is often easiest to ask first whether any individuals can be identified by the data they provide. This goes beyond just naming names; it includes contact information and demographic information that may be used to identify individuals as well. Imagine a student wants to collect data to see if her peers are satisfied with the intramural athletic program. As long as she did not ask for names and contact information, that would not require IRB approval because it is intended to evaluate a public program, not produce generalizable knowledge for her discipline. However, if she also collects data about personality traits that correlate with other responses, she is beginning to develop generalizable knowledge that could conceivably be presented or published. That latter activity is closer to the definition of research, so it would be best to proceed with IRB approval or at the very least, consult with the chair of the IRB.

PREPARING TO COMMUNICATE WITH THE IRB

If you believe your project needs to be reviewed, you should take some time to prepare before you start writing your proposal for the IRB. There are a few initial steps that should come as no surprise:

- You should be working with a faculty supervisor or mentor—make sure your mentor is involved in each step of the process.

- Design your research project based on accepted methods of your discipline— meeting scientific and ethical standards.

- Identify the requirements for your school's IRB, including specific forms to be completed and deadlines that should be met.

These basic steps will get you one step away from writing a review proposal for the IRB. Now, you may turn to the aspects of your study that the IRB will examine most closely. There are only a few steps in this process, but each requires your close attention.

What the IRB Needs to Know

The DHHS instructs IRB members to consider two things: the level of risk associated with your proposed research and the benefits of allowing the research to continue. Think about how medical researchers determine the effectiveness of new drugs for very serious illnesses: A sizeable portion of their participants will not receive any treatment at all, but will take a placebo instead. Here, the risk is that the illness is likely to run its course among the control group volunteers, at least for the duration of the study. The IRB members must approach this type of research looking for balance between the risk and benefit of each study. Specifically, for every increase in risk, there should be a noticeable increase in benefit as well. Make sure you understand the risks and benefits well enough to communicate them to the IRB.

Addressing the Risks and Benefits of Your Study

As a student researcher, you should not be designing life-or-death studies. Arguably, if you are a first-time researcher, you should be designing only studies with what is called **minimal risk**: *the likelihood of harm to a participant, and the severity of any harm that does happen, is no greater than what participants will encounter in their day-to-day activities or simple routine physical, psychological, or academic testing* (Department of Health and Human Services, 2009). If your research involves minimal risk—it does not add any risk to the average person's daily life—then your study may fall under the category of expedited review. **Expedited reviews** are *brief reviews of very low-risk research; these often are conducted by the chair of the IRB without involving the full committee.* If the chair agrees that your research is eligible for expedited review and approves of the project, then you can start your work much more quickly than if you waited for the full committee's review. When thinking about risks, consider all four categories of risks outlined in Chapter 4: physical harm, social harm, psychological harm, and punishment or liability. If any of these things are more likely to occur as a result of participating in your research, then you will need to address those concerns in your IRB application. If you cannot completely prevent them, then you will need full committee review.

Any researcher who thinks carefully about these categories should be able to identify the vast majority of risks. However, it might also be useful to ask yourself, "What would it be like to participate in my study?" Put yourself in the place of the volunteers you hope to test and run through your study. Can you see anything that might cause harm, or cause you to fear some sort of negative outcome? In order to do this, it is a good idea to start by writing out a research protocol.

Developing Your Research Protocol

In addition to developing operational definitions for your variables, you need to create a specific research plan called a **research protocol**, *a detailed description of the materials, methods, and activities involved in the proposed research.* In an experiment, this is your plan for how to assign participants to conditions or treatments, measure your variables, and control for confounding variables. Just as operational definitions clarify exactly how the variables in your study are manipulated and measured, protocols create a sort of definition for how you, your collaborators, and/or confederates will speak and behave during the study. This is not only a good way to identify the potential for risks, but it also adds to the validity and reliability of your study by reducing researcher bias. A completed protocol in some ways resembles an APA-style paper, and it includes the following:

- A brief preview of the purpose of the research and any specific research questions
- A review of the background research that leads to one or more hypotheses
- Procedures used to test the hypotheses, which include:
  o The population from which you will draw your sample(s)
  o Recruitment methods
  o Operational definitions; how you will measure or observe the behaviors
  o Step-by-step details about how you and your collaborators or research assistants will interact with participants
- An assessment of risks versus benefits, plus safeguards in place to reduce or prevent adverse events
- Timeline and plans for data collection and analysis
- A references page indicating the sources you have cited in your protocol

Despite similarities with an APA-style research report, protocols tend to offer significantly less information in the review of previous research and more in terms of the procedures that will be used. With a completed protocol in hand, you can more easily imagine what it would be like to participate in your own study—something the IRB will definitely need in order to evaluate your proposed research.

You will want to address your plans for maintaining confidentiality or anonymity of your participant's responses. If you recall Allen's study described in the opening to this chapter, he did not provide pure anonymity because he knew the identity of the persons he interviewed. He also failed to provide confidentiality because he provided information that would allow others to locate the participants. Anonymity and confidentiality are meant to protect individual participants in case their responses could damage their reputations or get them into trouble. Even if your study involves only minimal risk, it is still worthwhile to provide anonymity when you can; confidentiality of participants is always a requirement of human subjects research.

Preparing to Communicate With Your Participants

Communicating with participants involves a number of ethical procedures that demand close attention. Some things to consider are: How will you ensure that participants are fully informed and freely give consent? How will you ensure confidentiality and possibly, anonymity? How will you respond if something does go wrong? How will you debrief participants at the end of the study? These important topics were covered in Chapter 4 so they could receive significantly more attention. Here, we will focus on preparing materials for the IRB's consideration. In your IRB application, you will likely need to include:

- A statement used to recruit participants (e.g., an email, or a message posted online for student volunteers)

- A method of obtaining informed consent, most often a consent form that participants will sign. In cases of minimal risk, some IRBs are comfortable with an online consent statement preceding a survey

- Any instructions or scripted interaction with the participants that may introduce risk or deception

- Examples of feedback an individual may receive, such as test results or potentially diagnostic information

- Communication about whom to contact with questions or concerns

- A release statement in case you hope to share recordings or images of an individual (very rarely done)

- A debriefing statement that can be read to the participant, or printed so participants may keep a copy

During the review process, the IRB will want to make sure that you have appropriate procedures in place to address each of these bullet points. In addition, the IRB members will be evaluating the form of the communication to ensure that it is suitable for the audience. You will need to demonstrate that the actual language you use on the consent form and other documentation is at a reading level appropriate to your audience. Consider whether you are writing for the general population or for college students, who have a higher-than-average level of education. Adults who are new to your country may still be learning the language; this means that they likely have a less expansive vocabulary than native speakers and one that is more geared toward practical use (e.g., work, daily tasks) rather than abstract terminology used in research (e.g., *placebos, randomization*). Similarly, you will need to ensure that the concepts you describe are handled in a way that makes sense to individuals without exposure to your area of interest. Terms like *electroencephalogram* are likely to sound foreign and perhaps even scary to individuals unfamiliar with the tools of neuroscience. In either case—the extent of the vocabulary and familiarity with the concepts—the IRB will hold you, the researcher, responsible for ensuring that participants fully understand what they are volunteering to do.

WRITING YOUR IRB PROPOSAL

Now that you understand the role of the IRB in your research, have assessed the risks and how to reduce them, scripted a protocol to ensure you execute your plans ethically, and written out your communication with your participants, you can breathe a sigh of relief because the hard part is over. With all of these important elements in place, you simply have to communicate to the IRB by describing what you have just done, including the written examples for your protocol and communication with your volunteers. Before you begin, check one last time with your faculty advisor to make sure you are prepared; and if you are collaborating with other students, make sure they all agree on the materials and procedures your team has devised.

Writing for Your Audience

To this point, we have focused on the content of an IRB proposal. It may be less significant, but still very important to consider how you write your proposal in terms of addressing your audience and using the correct language and style. Part of this is simply to make sure the IRB can understand your research, even if they are unfamiliar with your topic. Before you start typing, remember that your audience—the members of the IRB— are most likely highly educated individuals. Even nonscientists on the IRB are likely to be familiar with the differences between an experimental and correlational design, and you can use research terms like those when appropriate. However, there is a very good chance that the topic you study is completely foreign to one, if not all, of the IRB members. Before you casually use terms like *salivary cortisol* or *self-determination theory*, you need to clearly define them and explain how they are essential to understanding your research.

In terms of language and style, most IRBs are willing to accept writing that is less formal than what you might submit for a final paper or a journal article. Nonetheless, it is good practice to produce something of very high quality. Your ability to communicate also says something about yourself. Imagine that there are significant social risks with a study that require careful attention to anonymity and confidentiality. If the IRB members receive a poorly written proposal with grammatical errors, typos, and lackluster organization, they may very well wonder if the researcher would be just as careless when implementing the procedures.

Following Up: Amending, Reporting, and Renewing

For some projects, the communication with the IRB will end once the approval is returned. However, there are situations in which you may find yourself contacting the IRB again. One reason is to amend your proposal due to changes in procedures, measurements, or communication with participants. For example, our students often contact the IRB after they have started data collection and realize that their proposed recruitment procedures are not generating enough participants; they often seek approval to recruit in new and different ways than they originally planned. Even the best-designed studies can go awry during the first few attempts at data collection, and the researcher will usually contact the IRB to fix a problem with the procedures. Similarly, researchers often come up with new hypotheses or ideas about design while they are conducting their study. If they design a new study with the same basic procedures, an *amendment* may be more reasonable that an entirely new proposal.

Amendments are generally much easier to write and review than original proposals; they are merely formal notes to the IRB about how the procedure will change. In some ways, an amendment is similar to the initial IRB proposal: most IRBs will have forms or instructions unique to its institution, and the IRB chair may determine that the change in protocol is exempt from further review (Resnik, Babson, & Dinse, 2012). As always, it is important to communicate with your faculty advisor about any changes you would like to make and with the IRB chair to see if an amendment is even necessary. For example, if you find that your simple questionnaire is just too long, it is probably not necessary to let the IRB know that you are removing 10 questions. Doing so does not add anything new to the study, and does not remove any of the safeguards against risk.

Another reason to contact the IRB during research is if, despite your best efforts, there is an **adverse event**, *an event during participation that negatively affects one or more participants in any way.* The IRB will need to keep a record of the incident and will need to review the procedures to determine whether there was a problem with the procedure, a failure to follow approved procedures, or some other unforeseen risk that had not been previously addressed.

Finally, long-running projects require researchers to keep the IRB up to date. For most institutions, the IRB asks for renewals or updates every 12 months, but it is well within their rights to ask for renewals and updates more frequently. In addition, the IRB will most likely ask that you complete a form or file a notice when the research is complete.

In some respects, this is the most practical chapter of the book. It draws on the ethical principles introduced and explained earlier—especially in Chapters 1 and 4—and describes the first steps in applying those principles. We encourage you to think of this chapter as an extension of those that came before rather than as something completely freestanding. That means you should review those earlier chapters to see the connections and paths from values, to ethical procedures, to implementation.

Chapter Summary

- In the US, universities are required to establish Institutional Review Boards (IRBs) to review, approve, and monitor all research activities involving human participants.

- For IRB purposes, research is defined as any systematic investigation designed to develop generalizable knowledge.

- Some activities that involve minimal risk are exempt from review or may qualify for expedited review.

- Researchers must write a protocol to address the potential risks and benefits of their proposed research. The IRB will only approve research if the potential benefits outweigh the risks.

- The researcher is responsible for keeping the IRB updated on any changes to an approved study or to any adverse events that occur.

Discussion Questions

1. The IRB regulations require the inclusion of individuals from multiple perspectives. What might be the reasons for including each type of representative on a board that reviews human subjects research proposals?

2. Identify the key ethical mistakes that Allen made when he started his research. And, what would the IRB require of him before he would be allowed to begin his interviewing?

3. Read the vignette below with the purpose and requirements for informed consent in mind:

   David Golding, a professor of counseling psychology, plans to conduct interviews and administer surveys to women in a shelter for domestic violence protection. His surveys will be online and will ask questions about the nature of the current abusive relationship and other relationships that may or may not have involved abuse and violence. In the interviews, he will be asking questions about the frequency, severity, and events preceding episodes of violence in the current relationship. He knows that there are numerous sensitive issues and responsibilities to women who volunteer to be in the study, so he seeks advice on how to construct the informed consent statement.

a. What types of risk are involved?

b. Do you have any suggestions for reducing those risks?

c. Do the benefits outweigh the risks?

d. Imagine that this research is proposed by a student researcher. Would that have any impact on how you would answer questions a or b? Explain.

Additional Resources

The Collaborative Institutional Training Initiative (CITI Program)

This organization provides online training directed toward human subjects research. CITI offers courses for a fee, but many colleges and universities have institutional subscriptions. In fact, some require their students and employees to complete CITI training before engaging in research with humans. Check with your research advisor about the availability of CITI training.

https://about.citiprogram.org/en/homepage/

Department of Health and Human Services, Office of Human Research Protections

The OHRP maintains and enforces regulations related to human subjects research in the United States. This site includes the regulations along with sections on education, participating in research, and determining whether your project needs review.

https://www.hhs.gov/ohrp/

National Institutes of Health (NIH) online training

NIH is the U.S. government's major provider of funding for biomedical research. Researchers who are awarded NIH grants must document human subjects training. This site provides online training course that will provide a certificate of completion. Like CITI training, it requires a fee but your university may have a program in place to pay for your registration.

https://phrp.nihtraining.com/users/login.php

References

Department of Health and Human Services. (2009). 45 CFR 46, Code of Federal Regulations. Retrieved from https://www.hhs.gov/ohrp/regulations-and-policy/regulations/45-cfr-46/index.html#46.107

Kallgren, C. A., & Tauber, R. T. (1996). Undergraduate research and the institutional review board: A mismatch or happy marriage? *Teaching of Psychology, 23*, 20–25.

Resnik, D. B., Babson, G., & Dinse, G. E. (2012). Minor changes to previously approved research: A study of IRB policies. *IRB, 34*, 9–14.

6

WORKING WITH ANIMAL SUBJECTS

Isaac was a student assistant in Dr. Warner's lab where they studied communication between domesticated dogs and humans. As a newcomer, Isaac had been put in charge of basic care, including the responsibility of providing food and water every evening. However, when a three-day weekend approached, Isaac decided to give the dogs twice as much food and water, thinking nobody would notice if he skipped a day. After all, the kennels had doors that allowed the dogs to come inside to rest or go out to their runs for exercise. While he was away, Isaac was surprised to get a phone call learning that two of the dogs had become extremely ill. It turns out that a hose filled with fluid for the ventilation system had been dripping slowly, and the dogs had been licking it up. Two things were clear: If the leak had been any worse, the dogs would have consumed a lethal dose. Further, had Isaac followed the research plan, he would have certainly found the problem sooner, saving the dogs from suffering.

In the 1950's, Russell and Burch authored *The Principles of Humane Experimental Technique*, one of the first and most influential academic works to address the use of animal subjects (Carbone, 2011; Ferdowsian & Beck, 2011). At that time, there was very little governmental or organizational oversight of animal-based research despite the fact that animals were widely used and welfare advocates were calling for humane treatment. The overarching principles introduced by Russell and Burch are now known as the three R's:

- Reduce the numbers of animals used as much as possible

- Refine methods to minimize distress and pain

- Replace animals with other research techniques when possible

Although they have been revised and expanded, the three R's are still relevant today and are the foundation for modern ethics guidelines regarding animal research.

RULES AND REGULATIONS FOR USE OF ANIMALS IN RESEARCH

In the United States, various scientific agencies collaborated to form the Interagency Research Animal Committee in 1985, which resulted in a report now commonly known as The Principles (its official title is *Principles for the Utilization and Care of Vertebrate Animals Used in Testing, Research, and Training*). This report serves as the basis for federal regulations regarding the treatment of research animals as set forth by the Animal Welfare Act (AWA, 7 U.S.C. §2131 et. seq.). The agency charged with overseeing and enforcing the AWA is the U.S. Department of Agriculture (USDA).

Federal regulations require research institutions to follow formal review procedures to protect animals. Similar to the IRBs described in Chapter 5, **Institutional Animal Care and Use Committees** (IACUC; often pronounced as the acronym EYE-yuh-kuk) *are committees formed at universities and other research centers to monitor the care and treatment of research animals.* Long before any research begins—before laboratory animals are even acquired—the IACUC ensures that the research facilities are able to accommodate animals humanely and safely. In addition to cages and other housing, facilities must have adequate temperature and ventilation controls, plumbing to allow for cleaning, and professionally trained caretakers.

Beyond the IACUC, there are limited federal regulations in place. Critics of the AWA say that it does not go far enough to protect animals, and their arguments have merit. The AWA protects only a small number of species—those that humans sense a connection with such as primates, dogs, and cats. Its policies do not address the treatment of reptiles or fish, nor the vast majority of all laboratory animals, mostly comprised of rats, mice, and other rodents (Latham, n.d.). For all of these species, including those covered by AWA, researchers follow the nonbinding regulations established by granting agencies such as the National Institutes of Health (National Research Council, 2011) and disciplinary organizations such as the American Psychological Association (APA, 2012). We believe the most ethical approach to research with animals—especially for student researchers—follows the more comprehensive guidelines that these groups offer. Therefore, we will draw primarily from CARE, the APA's Committee on Animals in Research and Education.

JUSTIFICATION OF RESEARCH

Ethical principles are meant to minimize distress or discomfort to the extent possible. One overarching theme in these principles is to assume any experience that would be painful or distressing for humans will likely be the same for most animals. A second theme is that, in contrast to human subjects, animal subjects cannot give informed consent. It is the job of the researchers along with the IACUC to decide whether the benefits of the research justify the discomfort or risk the animals will face. These principles require researchers to ask several questions before even acquiring animals to be used in research:

Purpose. Is the research driven by a "clear scientific purpose" (APA, 2012, p. 3), designed to produce knowledge on the development of species or individuals, normal functioning, disorders, or medical interventions?

Potential Impact. Will the outcome have a productive impact on the knowledge within a field? If so, is it expected to make theoretical and practical advances that will ultimately reduce suffering or improve the lives of humans and other animals?

Research Quality. Is the proposed research well-designed with adequate measures and controls in place? If not, the potential impact of the study is limited. Therefore, it becomes much more difficult to justify the procedures.

Lack of Alternatives. Is it possible to conduct similar high-impact research without animals? Perhaps it is possible to safely use human volunteers who are able to understand the risks and give informed consent. In some cases, there may be opportunities to use cultured cells or software models instead of living organisms.

These four areas represent the most significant ethical concepts that can be used to justify research with animals. However, there are also opposing questions that give context to the questions we just asked. What is the likelihood of pain or other distress? If the research does cause aversive reactions, how intense or prolonged is the experience? You can think of these as weights on a balance. For every degree of risk, the justifying answers should carry at least as much weight. In Isaac's example at the beginning of this chapter, the research was fairly easy to justify as it involved activities that the animals actually seem to enjoy and that do not pose any additional risks. Therefore, it would be justifiable even if it were a low-impact study. Certainly, however, there are psychological and biomedical studies for which a specific type of discomfort is actually the purpose of the experiment—research on pain, illness, and medical treatments, for example. These are the studies that require a high probability of making a significant contribution to the field to justify the study.

There is one last consideration of particular relevance to us as students and teachers: the use of animals for educational purposes. The balance analogy relies on the strength of the research to offset the risk to animals. In purely educational settings, there is minimal chance of producing significant scientific knowledge, so there can be almost no risk and only very minimal discomfort to the animals, such as a day of food deprivation or the mildest of electrical shocks. A good test of ethical treatment here is to ask, "Would I be willing to experience this treatment if it provided a good educational experience?" In fact, the APA recommends that, when possible, all researchers should try the procedure to understand the level of discomfort involved. Finally, the educational use of animals should include instruction about the ethics presented in this chapter. And, because these activities require the same handling and care as in actual research, the IACUC will need to review facilities and procedures.

The principles involved in justification of research are important to understand and follow. However, they are not a complete set of ethics: These elements of animal research are abstract and often rely on predictions about what the research may do in the future. These ethics do not deal with the physical, day-to-day experiences the animals will have. Thus, further principles must address the capabilities of the researcher and the physical environment to carry out the research as planned.

CAPABILITIES OF THE PERSONNEL AND INSTITUTION

In hypothetical situations, ethical judgments can be made entirely on the principles we outlined above. However, the world in which the experiments actually take place is not as simple. Researchers can make mistakes; inadequate housing and care can lead to distress to the animals than the research itself. Therefore, it is just as important to examine the context of the research as it is the justification on scientific grounds.

In order to provide some context, consider an experiment that involves administering a powerful stimulant drug to rats. Ethical research demands that the research team include at least one person trained and experienced in the specific drug, its dosage, signs of overdose or adverse reactions, and the prevention and control of infections. Some drugs of this type, such as methamphetamine, also require government-issued licenses. Obviously, this particular type of research is going to be out of reach for undergraduates and even most graduate students who design and conduct their own studies. On the other hand, students in some fields of neuroscience and physiological psychology may very well find themselves working in a lab on these types of projects. Although that is unlikely for most students, there are a number of very mundane issues that all animal-based studies will involve.

Competence. All researchers need a minimal level of competence related to daily lab operations and the research procedures. This can be as simple as knowing how to use thermostats, lighting, and operant conditioning chambers. Imagine what could happen if an assistant does not fully understand how to use equipment: A mishandled rat may escape, incorrectly operated thermostats may lead to hypothermia, and electrode with too much current could seriously harm an animal subject. Accidents can happen at any time with well-trained researchers, but allowing poorly trained, inexperienced assistants to work unsupervised on these tasks is more negligent than accidental. The ethical responsibility falls on the supervising researchers to judge their own competence before taking on a project, and to train all workers in their laboratories to understand and operate the equipment.

Expertise with species. All members of a research team should be trained to work with the species. Again, this begins with daily care (amount and type of food required; sensitivity to temperatures) to experimental procedures (recognizing species-specific behaviors, especially those indicating distress). What if Isaac had approached the dogs he was caring for and they all remained lying on their sides? Is that typical for this breed, or these individuals? Or, do they usually greet people with excitement? Understanding and paying attention to the unique behaviors of the species or breed is one of the best ways to prevent adverse events.

Ethical acquisition and transport. Students are rarely, if ever, charged with finding lab animals, but it is worth knowing that there are standards in this area as well. Animals should be either bred in the lab or acquired from companies or individuals that have the expertise described above. Ethical responsibilities begin there and continue throughout the entire time the animal is in the researcher's possession.

Care and feeding. Animals should be housed in ways that promote well-being, with enough space, social contact, food, and water. They should be handled gently and provided veterinary care if needed. Notice that this particular set of obligations goes beyond the people working with the animals; it also requires a physical space and equipment that are suitable to the species. For this reason, the IACUC will review facilities on a regular basis, not just when considering proposed experimental procedures.

Terminating the research. Researchers have a number of responsibilities to the animals even after the research has been completed. This includes the issues listed above, such as housing, but now includes decisions about what happens to the animals. The most preferable option would be to continue with additional ethical research using the same animals. Most animal-based research involves animals that have been bred and born in a laboratory setting. These animals should not be released into the wild because most are not prepared for it, and it would likely have undesirable consequences for the ecosystem. Finally, there are some forms of research that require euthanasia. The techniques used should be quick and cause as little pain as possible, requiring the expertise and other capabilities described above.

TABLE 6.1 ■ Specific Ethical Responsibilities for Students and Their Mentors	
Mentor Responsibilities	**Student Responsibilities**
• Explain the purpose of the research and why it is considered to be justifiable.	• Read recommended literature and ask questions.
• Explain and demonstrate methods for feeding, cleaning, and handling the species.	• Ask questions to make sure you understand procedures.
• Explain the experimental procedures, including how to handle the animals, ensure safety and comfort to the degree possible, and what risks might be present.	• Practice the procedures with a mentor or experienced assistants present. • Follow procedures; do not take shortcuts.
• Describe warning signs that the animals are experiencing unexpected levels of stress.	• Do not make assumptions about what might happen if you change procedures or skip steps.
• Describe indicators that research equipment or other physical resources are not working as planned.	• Test yourself to make sure you can make judgments about risk and what steps to take if problems arise. • Report any problems or concerns to a supervisor or mentor immediately.

Note that these principles address the abilities of the researcher, but personality and work ethic are every bit as important here. In Isaac's example, he had the knowledge, experience, and ability to care for the animals. The ethical problem here is that Isaac took a shortcut and did not follow the specified procedure. By making the decision himself without consulting his research mentor or lab supervisor, he failed to meet his ethical responsibilities. To summarize, all individuals involved must behave according to instructions and follow through on all assigned tasks. Each individual is responsible for knowing the risk factors and any warning signs from the animals or equipment that signal increased risk and unintended pain or injury.

THE STUDENT RESEARCHER

There are specific ethical responsibilities of students and their research mentors when using animals in research. We have summarized those in Table 6.1. Compared to research with humans, there are few governmental regulations and little oversight of animal subjects. Nonetheless, some researchers who have supervised students in both contexts tell us that it can be more difficult to train students to conduct animal research than to complete similar procedures with humans. This is anecdotal, so we cannot say whether it is true everywhere, but it is interesting to think about why some researchers would form such an opinion. It could be due in part to the fact that animals need housing and feeding, whereas most human-based studies require only temporary contact. Additionally, once humans give informed consent, they are able to alert researchers to problems, discomfort, and so forth, and even to withdraw from the study if they choose. Finally, most students are not familiar with mice, rats, and other animals that make up the majority of lab subjects. For all these reasons, students involved in animal research are more likely to be considered research assistants or lab technicians rather than independent researchers with faculty supervision.

In terms of educational value, it is beneficial to understand when and why animal research is justifiable, but the actual ethical responsibilities relate to their tasks and procedures. Faculty have the responsibility of educating students on the general ethical principles as well as the specifics for the care and feeding of the species and the humane treatment of subjects during handling and testing.

Chapter Summary

- The three R's summarize the theme of animal research ethics: Reduce, refine, and replace.

- In the United States, the Department of Agriculture enforces federal regulations for animal research. However, those regulations are quite limited.

- Research procedures and the basic care of animals must be reviewed and approved by a university's Institutional Animal Care and Use Committee (IACUC).

- An IACUC may approve research if the pain and risks are justified by the potential scientific impact.

- Ethical principles dictate that the facilities are suitable for the animals' health and that all members of the research team know how to care for the species they study.

- The principles require extra responsibilities in animal research due to the fact that, unlike humans, animal subjects need housing and feeding. In addition, humans can give informed consent and alert the researchers to problems, whereas animals cannot.

Discussion Questions

1. Reread Isaac's story at the beginning of the chapter, and then review the major responsibilities outlined in the three sections. What principles are most relevant to the situation: Those related to *Justification*? *Capabilities*? *Student or Mentor Responsibilities*? Explain.

2. The principles described here are meant to be minimal standards. Some researchers and members of the general public think they are not strong enough. What is your opinion? Are there any other provisions you believe should be added?

3. Imagine you are a member of your university's IACUC and you have been presented with a proposal describing the following situation:

   Dr. Zafran is examining some promising new behavioral treatments for reducing and coping with symptoms of post-acute withdrawal syndrome (PAWS) for alcohol-dependent individuals. These symptoms include tremors, mood swings, insomnia, and confusion lasting for months after alcohol consumption has completely stopped. Unlike acute withdrawal, better known as a hangover, PAWS occurs only among people who have become physically dependent on alcohol after years of nearly nonstop drinking. Because of the risk of irreversible brain and liver damage in adults, or even immediate death, Dr. Zafran has chosen to use an animal model of PAWS in which she experimentally creates the symptoms of PAWS. She acknowledges the fact that the rats experience discomfort and are then euthanized, but wonders whether her undergraduate student, Reyna, should be allowed to design and conduct her own study using the same basic procedures.

   a. Refer to the *Justification* section and identify specific principles that are relevant. How might Dr. Zafran use these to justify her own work? Are there additional things you might look for in the proposal or question Dr. Zafran about before making your final decision? Might these apply in the same way to her student, who is using the same basic methods?

   b. Using the PASA model, think about whether you believe it is justifiable for Reyna to develop her own study using similar procedures and with similar consequences for the rats. What would be the most appropriate approach: Allow Reyna to go on as she planned, revise her procedures substantially, or give up on that idea completely and work on a topic that does not involve animals? (The *Capabilities* and *Student–Mentor* sections would be helpful here.)

Additional Resources

The American Association for Laboratory Animal Science

The AALAS is an interdisciplinary organization that promotes ethical treatment of laboratory animals and provides support to researchers. The association hosts a comprehensive and useful website called IACUC central: https://www.aalas.org/iacuc

American Psychological Association Committee on Animal Research and Ethics

The APA provides discipline-specific guidelines that reinforce and supplement U.S. governmental standards: http://www.apa.org/science/leadership/care/guidelines.aspx

The Hastings Center

Latham has written an interesting overview of animal research ethics and offers insight into why the principles exist and how they may or may not be effective.

http://animalresearch.thehastingscenter.org/report/u-s-law-and-animal-experimentation-a-critical-primer/

U.S. Animal Welfare Act

The national standards in the United States can be read as an e-book: https://www.ncbi .nlm.nih.gov/books/NBK54050. Look for the links on the side of this web page to view the book in various formats, including a PDF for downloads.

The standards for many other countries are easy to find with a quick web search.

References

American Psychological Association. (2012). *Guidelines for ethical conduct in the care and use of nonhuman animals in research*. Retrieved from http://www.apa.org/ science/leadership/care/guidelines.aspx

Carbone, L. (2011). Pain in laboratory animals: The ethical and regulatory imperatives. *PLOS One, 6*(9), e21578.

Ferdowsian, H. R., & Beck, N. (2011). Ethical and scientific considerations regarding animal testing and research. *PLOS One, 6*(9), e24059.

Latham, S. J. (n.d.). *Ethics of medical research with animals: Science, values, and alternatives*. Retrieved from http://animalresearch.thehastingscenter.org/report/u-s-law-and-animal-experimentation-a-critical-primer

National Research Council. (2011). *Guide for the care and use of laboratory animals* (8th ed.). Washington, DC: National Academies Press. Retrieved from www.ncbi.nlm .nih.gov/books/NBK54050.

7

RESEARCH MISCONDUCT

Zahra, Jameson, and Vincent are working on a research project with their professor studying psychological sense of community among different groups at a large university. Part of their work is to go out in public to conduct surveys with students, faculty, and staff who are willing to answer questions for a few minutes. Unfortunately, recruiting participants has been challenging because of the amount of time it takes and because participants do not receive anything for their efforts. The three student researchers collected the first round of data at a football game and got a 10% response rate. They planned to meet at several more campus events over the next week and then collate their data. Although Vincent did not show up as they had planned, he returned Monday with 50 completed surveys. Zahra told Jameson that she was suspicious—how was Vincent able to get so many surveys in so few days? Vincent claimed to have attended a couple of smaller events over the weekend but was vague about the details. His collaborators were skeptical and torn about what to do. They were relieved to have enough data to run the analyses the professor was expecting; however, they also had reason to believe Vincent had made up some of the data to meet their goal.

What should Zahra and Jameson do about their concerns? Is there really any harm in making up data just to get through a student research project? If, in fact, Vincent made up data, he has violated research ethics and the responsible conduct of research. This is a form of **research misconduct,** a *willful violation of research ethics intended to* *deceive others into accepting false information.* Acts of misconduct, such as creating fake data or claiming another researcher's work as one's own, can potentially lead to harmful outcomes and is unfair to other researchers who behave conscientiously and ethically.

RESEARCH MISCONDUCT

The Office of Research Integrity (ORI) in the U.S. Department of Health and Human Services is responsible for protecting the rights and welfare of human participants involved in research conducted or supported by the government and its agencies (see Chapters 4 and 5 for details of those regulations). Although this is what the ORI is best known for, it also handles cases of research misconduct that relate directly to treatment of human or animal subjects. Specific instances of research misconduct include (Public Health Service, 2005) "fabrication, falsification, or plagiarism [often referred to as *FFP*] in proposing, performing, or reviewing research, or in reporting research results:

(a) *Fabrication* is making up data or results and recording or reporting them.

(b) *Falsification* is manipulating research materials, equipment, or processes, or changing or omitting data or results such that the research is not accurately represented in the research record.

(c) *Plagiarism* is the use of another person's ideas, processes, results, or words without giving appropriate credit.

(d) Research misconduct does not include honest error or differences of opinion."

Research misconduct also includes violations concerning breaches of confidentiality (see Chapters 2 and 3) and publication (see Chapter 9). In all of these cases, the actions are considered research misconduct whether it is committed intentionally and willingly, through negligence and carelessness, or even through a failure to understand the regulations and what is acceptable.

In this chapter, we focus on fabrication and falsification as well as explore questionable research practices. Plagiarism is, unfortunately, both a serious and common ethical violation and deserves an in-depth discussion. Students often struggle to understand the various forms of plagiarism and how to avoid them. Therefore, Chapter 9–*Ethical Writing Practices* gives special attention to plagiarism. For now, we will focus on research practices that violate scientific integrity.

RESEARCH MISCONDUCT IS HARMFUL

Two of the ethical principles applied throughout this book—beneficence and nonmaleficence—promote the well-being of others and avoid doing harm. It is easy to think of these principles as they relate to the treatment of research participants. However, all forms of research misconduct undermine these ethical principles and the values of scientific inquiry. To get some perspective, think about this analogy with medicine:

Failure to conduct research ethically will "contaminate the literature with nonreplicable, misestimated, or spurious findings . . . . Like medical professionals who fail to wash their hands despite knowing it to be a best practice, behavior scientists who decide not to take even minimal steps to improve their practice are doing harm to our discipline from inside" (Osborne, 2017, p. 154).

For professional researchers, fabricating and falsifying research signifies a breach of trust with the scientific community and with the public who depends on science. In practical terms, this form of research misconduct has two main effects:

- *Misuse of resources.* False results lead other researchers to waste time and resources in attempts to reproduce and extend findings that were, in reality, fabricated.

- *Adopting unsupported treatments.* False results can lead people to rely on psychological interventions, medical treatments, and other applications that have little to no benefit while diverting efforts away from treatments and applications that are effective.

Both of these effects illustrate how fabrication is inconsistent with the principles of beneficence and nonmaleficence: Falsification does not help anyone and, at times, it can actually cause harm.

The case of Dr. Andrew Wakefield illustrates both ill effects that arise from falsified data. In 1998, a prestigious journal, *The Lancet*, published Wakefield's paper in which he attempted to establish a causal link between the MMR (measles-mumps-rubella) vaccination and diagnosis of autism. When some inconsistencies came to light, a medical panel reviewed Wakefield's research. The investigation revealed a financial conflict of interest along with falsified data. This is a very clear case of research misconduct, and a problem that you might think would be easy to correct. However, the negative effects of falsification linger on. The application of Wakefield's false findings has caused harm: It contributed to decreasing vaccination rates in Britain and the United States (Gallagher, 2015). Although the drop in vaccination rates has done nothing to reduce the incidence of autism, it has caused a resurgence in illnesses and death due to preventable diseases. This includes record numbers of measles cases in 2014, which is surprising considering that the disease was reported to be eliminated in the United States in 2000 (CDC, 2018).

Wakefield's misconduct has also contributed to the waste of resources spent countering his bogus claims. For example, one recent *meta-analysis* (a statistical technique used to combine research findings from multiple studies) that included 1.2 million children did not find any increased risk of autism associated with the MMR vaccination (Taylor, Swerdfeger, & Eslick, 2014). In fact, the researchers reported a slight decreased risk of autism in children who received the MMR vaccination. This is one example of how researchers spend time and money to re-establish the benefits of vaccination, a practice that had already been supported by substantial laboratory research and decades of public health records. Although this is valuable research, the need for continued work on this topic means that resources are not being spent on preventions, treatments, and cures for a number of other diagnosed conditions.

Falsification and fabrication cases generally do not contribute to such large-scale public health issues, nor is it so difficult to prevent the spread of the falsified conclusions. When journal editors do learn of falsified or fabricated data in their publications, they will issue a **retraction,** a *statement from the editorial board that nullifies and rejects the* *original publication.* It is not possible to gather up the copies that are already in print, but journals can use their website, news outlets, and newsletters in professional organizations to publicize that they no longer stand behind the research. One of the best resources for students to learn about recently retracted publications is *Retraction Watch*, an organization committed to integrity in science publishing. Their website describes ongoing investigations and recently resolved cases from a wide range of disciplines.

The good news is that serious research misconduct, such as fabrication and falsification of data and results, does not occur very often (Fanelli, 2009; Gordon, 2014). A recent study that asked researchers directly about misconduct found that 0.3% to 4.9% of scientists admitted to falsifying or fabricating data (Fanelli, 2009). However, when scientists were asked about less serious, but questionable, research practices, such as leaving out data, changing the design of a study, or changing reported results, up to 33.7% of scientists admitted to some of these behaviors. These **questionable research practices** (QRPs), *actions on the part of the researcher that can lead to false impressions about a study and reduce replicability*, are more common than FFP but nonetheless problematic.

QUESTIONABLE RESEARCH PRACTICES

Scientists must make many decisions throughout the research process. These decisions are informed by their discipline, methods, training, and experience. What are the best experimental designs and measures to test this hypothesis? What type of statistical test is appropriate, and is it OK to remove data from participants with unusually high or low scores? What if you need to change your research protocol after the IRB has approved it? In some cases, the decisions that scientists make lead to questionable research practices (de Vries, Anderson, & Martinson, 2006). Examples of QRPs include poor record keeping, removing data or cases that do not support the hypotheses, failing to correct errors in the data or results, failing to report all of the conditions in an experiment, rounding down *p* values, changing hypotheses to match the outcomes, and leaving out details of the methodology (John, Loewenstein, & Prelec, 2012). It is more difficult to detect QRPs than outright fabrication and falsification (Gordon, 2014). As you learned in Chapter 5, IRBs are focused on the ethical treatment of research subjects. They do not monitor and evaluate methodological issues, statistical analyses, or the maintenance and storage of data files inasmuch as they do not violate participants' rights. Just because the IRB does not monitor QRPs, does not mean that researchers can engage in these ethical violations. In Table 7.1, we have listed some common QRPs and best practices to avoid them.

Professional scientists are often under pressure to support their hypotheses so that their research will be published or their grants renewed. Professionals have other incentives for publishing as well: advancement in one's career and reputation, access to more grants and funding for research, and opportunities for speaking engagements and book contracts. Adding to the pressure to publish is the **publication bias**, the increased likelihood that scientific journals will publish studies with multiple, statistically significant findings while rejecting manuscripts that describe nonsignificant results. It follows, then, that a successful career requires researchers to find statistically significant results, regularly and often. With that kind of pressure, you can imagine the temptation

TABLE 7.1 ■

Questionable Research Practices	Best Practices to Avoid Misconduct
RESEARCH PROTOCOL	
Changing research hypotheses as you collect data	Create a research proposal before you begin and preregister your study
Failing to report all of the variables measured in the study	Report all independent and dependent variables
Changing the research protocol to make data collection faster or easier	Follow the approved IRB protocol; contact IRB if you need to make changes to your data collection procedures
DATA MANAGEMENT & STORAGE	
Throwing out original, physical research documents, such as questionnaires, recordings, or data sheets	Maintain original research documents, surveys, and recordings in a secure location for a specified time period
Failing to save a copy of the original, raw data files in digital format	Save raw data with appropriate file names in a password-protected drive. Backup files in secure location when possible.
Losing original data files	Give your research supervisor a copy of the original data or data file
Recoding or changing data points	Submit a data management plan to your research supervisor *before* you recode or analyze the data
DATA ANALYSIS	
Deleting data points that look like outliers	Use specific, predetermined criteria to eliminate data points, for example, three standard deviations from the mean
Collecting just enough data to support your hypothesis and then stopping	Use a power analysis to set the number of participants before you begin the study
Conducting different statistical tests until you get the result you expected, or other results that may help you present or publish your data	Choose which statistical tests to run *before* you collect data
Rounding down *p* values	Report exact *p* values as calculated
SHARING RESULTS	
Reporting only results that support your hypotheses	Report all results that are relevant to your hypotheses
Withholding details of the methodology	Include a detailed methodology in your paper
Not reporting all of the conditions or dependent variables	Identify all of the conditions of the experiment and all variables measured, even if not all data will be relevant to your hypotheses. You do not have to report findings for data that are not relevant.

to bend the rules a little—in other words, engage in QRPs—to get your data to say what you want them to. We see a similar trend among our students who often feel that nonsignificant results mean that their project is unsuccessful and that they might face a grade penalty for not supporting their hypothesis. They, too, feel the pressure to conduct solid research, achieve high grades, and build a strong graduate school application. We emphasize the quality of the research design, data analysis, and interpretation over supporting a hypothesis.

Errors: Honest and Otherwise

Researchers must accept that honest errors and mistakes can happen and should be corrected as soon as possible. The results of these mistakes may resemble those that occur in deliberate acts of research misconduct, or they may be genuine mistakes that occur when researchers are negligent or reckless in how they manage the data collection, analysis, and reporting. Both misconduct and carelessness are damaging to science, but honest mistakes can occur as well. For example, one recent study was questioned when the authors reported incorrect statistics; the reported F values did not correspond with the correct p values. Once the error was discovered, the journal editors investigated and quickly realized they had not made all of the author's corrections before sending the finished manuscript for publication. Mistakes like these are bound to happen in long, complex processes that involve many different people—like publishing an article—despite very careful proofreading. Unfortunately, the differences between deliberate misconduct and honest mistakes are not always clear. One recent study found that a little over 10% of research articles published in a sample of major psychology journals reported an incorrect p value, similar to what is described in the example (Nuijtin, Hartgerink, van Assen, Epskamp, & Wicherts, 2015). However, the researchers also found that incorrect p values were more likely to be reported as significant than nonsignificant, offering further evidence of publication bias.

Mistakes like these are considered reporting errors; honest mistakes and errors that are corrected are not considered research misconduct. The peer review process will often catch these mistakes before the results are made public. **Peer review** is *the process by which other scientists with similar research interests are asked to review a study before it is published*. These peers are tasked with evaluating the quality of the research conducted to ensure that the methodology and data analysis are consistent with accepted practices in the discipline as well as to evaluate the study's findings and conclusions. Peer review is integral to the research process and is covered in more detail in Chapter 9. We find it helpful for students to practice peer review with each other. It can be a useful learning experience and often makes students better writers as they learn the challenges of communicating ideas clearly and accurately.

Replication

Another avenue in which errors or even serious misconduct can be identified is through the research replication process. To facilitate replication, scientists openly describe their research methods and analyses in enough detail so that other scientists can retest those same hypotheses. If research findings can be reproduced, then they will be more widely accepted. When replication produces different results than the originally published work, we must ask whether the hypothesis is incorrect. If so, did the original researchers engage in misconduct, or did they employ QRPs? If one fails to replicate a study, it does not necessarily mean that research misconduct has occurred. However, a more detailed review of the methods may be necessary to determine why the results could not be replicated.

The Collaborative Replications and Education Project (CREP) is a great resource for undergraduate students and their research mentors. CREP is a replication program that allows student researchers to collaborate on larger projects by contributing data samples to ongoing projects. Because undergraduate students do not often replicate their own work, collaborating with other groups of students to replicate previous studies is a great way to learn about research ethics and the open science framework.

HANDLING RESEARCH MISCONDUCT

The federal government is responsible for oversight of research misconduct in cases in which the researcher has received federal funds or grants. Institutions, such as colleges and universities, are responsible for the research conducted by their employees. This includes ensuring the responsible conduct of research and handling cases of research misconduct. Instructors, and in some cases research assistants, are responsible for overseeing the activities of student researchers. Universities usually have a **research integrity officer,** *a member of the institution who oversees inquiries or investigations into allegations of research misconduct* and generally follows the procedures outlined by the Office of Research Integrity (Public Health Service, 2005):
"A finding of research misconduct requires that:

(a) There be a significant departure from accepted practices of the relevant research community;

(b) The misconduct be committed intentionally, knowingly, or recklessly; and

(c) The allegation be proven by a preponderance of the evidence."

Institutions should have clear policies and procedures in place to handle instances of research misconduct. Again, these misconduct policies are primarily directed at faculty, staff, and graduate students who are more likely to be conducting research than undergraduate students. Some institutions have a separate policy for handling research misconduct by undergraduates; it is often under the student conduct or academic integrity policy.

CONSEQUENCES OF RESEARCH MISCONDUCT

There have been some rather high profile cases recently that shed light on how misconduct is handled at research institutions. In August of 2017, Ohio State University (OSU) revoked the PhD of a recent doctoral student who coauthored a paper with a faculty member while she was a graduate student. The study examined the effect of first-person shooter video games on accuracy of real-life shooting. The study reported that participants who played a violent shooting game that rewarded shots in the head of a human-like target got 99% more headshots when using a realistic pistol aimed at a mannequin (Whitaker & Bushman, 2014). It also reported that habitual use of violent video games increased accuracy of shooting. Two researchers who study the relationship between violent video games and behavior notified the OSU that there were "irregularities" in the data. The study's authors turned the data files over to be examined. Although OSU will not share the details of their investigation, two things emerged. First, the OSU professor agreed to a retraction of the study. Second, there was a research misconduct investigation launched by OSU that ended in a revocation of the PhD of the recent graduate student. The reported irregularities in the data stemmed from the existence of two data files. The two data files were different, but it was unclear which one was the original or raw data. Given the two different data files, it appeared to investigators that data was altered to support the study's hypotheses.

What happens to faculty who are found guilty of research misconduct? Depending on the severity of misconduct and how many instances are uncovered, some researchers may lose their grant money and others may lose their jobs. More commonly, a study is retracted and the researcher faces penalties such as unpaid leave or required supervision. At the same time, their peers and students may be reluctant to collaborate or work for that individual—why put yourself at risk for being accused of misconduct?

Graduate student researchers also face stiff penalties because they are expected to know and understand the ethical principles involved in the conduct of research. They are often collaborating with faculty and peers and are likely to be dismissed from working on current projects and excluded from others. Formal penalties for graduate students vary from being removed from a research project or lab to being suspended or expelled from their program. With regard to undergraduate students, many institutions consider research misconduct under the broader category of *academic misconduct,* which includes violations such as cheating and plagiarism. Often undergraduates are conducting research for academic credit, so it makes sense to treat research misconduct as a type of cheating.

Student researchers are solely responsible for their own decisions and actions, but a research mentor or supervisor is responsible for ensuring students have proper training for the work they are conducting in the research project. It is difficult to know the consequences of research misconduct for undergraduates because these incidents may be dealt with one-on-one, within a department, or in a student conduct hearing. Unless an undergraduate student is working on a federal grant, research misconduct likely goes unreported beyond the department or administration.

Let's wrap up our discussion of research misconduct by revisiting the scenario at the beginning of the chapter. Jameson and Zahra suspect that their research partner may have fabricated data; what should they do? A charge of research misconduct is very serious. Think back to our discussion of the values of collaborative research—trust, honesty, fairness, and accountability. What are these students' responsibilities to each other, their research supervisor, and the scientific community? We recommend that they share their concerns immediately with their professor. The professor should be familiar with the research misconduct or integrity policy that applies to the situation and be able to explain what type of documentation or evidence is appropriate to move forward with an inquiry into the misconduct. It is the responsibility of the research supervisor to discuss the concerns of the research team members with Vincent and ask for the data. If the raw data cannot be produced, an investigation into misconduct should commence.

Chapter Summary

- Research misconduct is a violation of research ethics intended to deceive others into accepting false or inaccurate information.
- The main categories of research misconduct are fabrication, falsification, and plagiarism.
- Less serious forms of misconduct, referred to as questionable research practices, are far more common, but still pose a threat to scientific integrity.
- Honest errors do sometimes occur but can often be identified through the peer review process.
- The federal government and universities have developed misconduct policies to deal with cases of research misconduct.
- The consequences of engaging in research misconduct can be serious and range from the retraction of a study and loss of research funds to being fired. Students may face repercussions in the form of grades or disciplinary actions.

Discussion Questions

1. As part of their senior research project, two psychology students are studying the effects of chronotype (i.e., being a morning lark versus a night owl) on moral decision making. They need half of their participants to be morning larks, which is difficult to find on a college campus. To further complicate matters, they need to test half of the morning larks late at night when they are out of sync with their biological rhythms. Because they cannot recruit enough participants who meet the chronotype score for a morning lark, they decide to adjust the cut-off scores for morning larks to create an even number of participants in each condition.

   a. Do you believe there are any ethical issues (or potential for ethical issues) with creating their own cut-off score? Why or why not?

   b. If you do believe there are ethical issues, are there any ways to justify their decision to adjust the cut-off?

2. In the case of the "Head Shots" video game research, what is the harm of making up or falsifying data to support the hypothesis? How might the findings from that study be applied or used in real-life settings?

3. Does your school have a research misconduct policy? Does it include undergraduate and graduate students? If so, what is the first thing you should do if you suspect misconduct has occurred?

Additional Resources

Collaborative Replications and Education Project (CREP)

CREP is a replication program for student researchers that allows them to collaborate on larger projects by contributing data samples to ongoing projects.

https://osf.io/flaue/

Resources for Research Ethics and Education

The Research Ethics Program at UC San Diego created a project to promote the responsible conduct of research through best practices and evidence-based education in research ethics. This website offers a helpful overview of research ethics.

http://research-ethics.net

Retraction Watch

Retraction Watch is an organization that monitors and reports on published research that has been retracted due to a finding of research misconduct. Retraction Watch is part of the Center for Scientific Integrity whose mission is to promote transparency and integrity in science and scientific publishing.

http://retractionwatch.com/

References

Centers for Disease Control and Prevention. (2018). *Measles cases and outbreaks*. U.S. Department of Health and Human Service. Retrieved from https://www.cdc.gov/measles/cases-outbreaks.html

de Vries, R., Anderson, M. S., & Martinson, B. A. (2006). Normal misbehavior: Scientists talk about the ethics of research. *Journal of Empirical Research on Human Research Ethics: An International Journal*, *1*, 43–50.

Fanelli, D. (2009). How many scientists fabricate and falsify research? A systematic review and meta-analysis of survey data. *PLoS ONE*, *4*(5), e5738.

Gallagher, J. (2015, September 23). *Childhood MMR vaccination rates fall*. BBC News website. Retrieved from http://www.bbc.com/news/health-34335509

Gordon, A. (2014). Rational choice and moral decision making in science. *Ethics & Behavior*, *24*, 175–194.

John, L. K., Loewenstein, G., & Prelec, D. (2012). Measuring the prevalence of questionable research practices with incentives for truth telling. *Psychological Science*, *23*(5), 524–532.

Nuijtin, M. B., Hartgerink, C. H. J., van Assen, M. A. L. M., Epskamp, S., & Wicherts, J. M. (2015). The prevalence of statistical reporting errors in psychology (1985–2013). *Behavior Research Methods*, *48*, 1205–1226.

Osborne, J. W. (2017). Best practices: A moral imperative. *Canadian Journal of Behavioral Science*, *49*, 153–158.

Public Health Service. (2005). *Policies on research misconduct*. Retrieved from https://ori.hhs.gov/FR_Doc_05-9643

Taylor, L. E., Swerdfeger, A. L., & Eslick, G. D. (2014). Vaccines are not related to autism: An evidence-based meta-analysis of case-control and cohort studies. *Vaccine*, *32*(29), 3623–3629.

Whitaker, J. L., & Bushman, B. J. (2014). Boom, Headshot!: Effect of video game play and controller type on firing aim and accuracy. *Communication Research*, *41*, 879–891.

8

ETHICS OF STATISTICAL PRACTICES

Kayla completed an original study on perceptions of cell phone users for her capstone course. Her participants acted as employers, conducting mock interviews of confederates in three conditions: one confederate held a cell phone during the exchange, another laid a phone on the table, and a third said, "Excuse me" and made a show of stowing the phone in a backpack. Her mentor rated the paper as an A, praising it for its clearly stated hypothesis and sound methods that produced statistically significant results—participants rated the candidate with the backpack higher than the other two. Later, when Kayla was putting together a conference presentation, she needed assistance creating a graph of her results. Kayla's mentor loaded the spreadsheet into the statistics software and attempted to reproduce the analysis. However, she found different results— the numbers were far from statistically significant. When pressed, Kayla insisted that she had not fabricated the results, although she acknowledged that she made some adjustments to the data, conducting a series of ANOVA tests after each adjustment: She deleted one participant who was an outlier, having given everyone terrible ratings, and another when the confederate's cell phone rang inside the backpack. After finding that the overall rating of the confederate was not significant, she broke it down into its components: "professionalism" did produce a significant ANOVA whereas "would recommend for hiring" did not. The result of these adjustments was the significant finding she planned to present, although neither her paper nor the draft of her presentation made any mention of the steps she took along the way.

D o you believe Kayla did something unethical, or even engaged in outright lying? In this particular case, Kayla insisted that she did not cheat—she was simply using procedures she had learned in her statistics class and had observed her mentor use during their previous research collaboration. If that is true, then perhaps she made an honest mistake and misunderstood how her mentor has been conducting analyses. Which is it: Did Kayla fabricate or falsify the data, or did she just misunderstand the procedures?

In this chapter, we will find that a third scenario is quite likely: Kayla analyzed data that were collected honestly and accurately using modifications that she had seen others use in the past. We will explore how the source of this problem arises from commonly used practices that have only recently begun to be viewed as unethical: a problem that emphasizes the need for self-discipline, honesty, openness, and full disclosure of research methods.

STATISTICS IN RESEARCH

If you are ready to engage in research, then you are certainly aware that statistics will play a central role in understanding your results. Most likely, you have completed at least one course on statistics, or you may be even enrolled in a statistics or research methods course right now. This chapter is aimed at students with enough experience to know what a z-test or t-test is meant to accomplish and the understanding that factors, such as sample size, can have a big effect on the outcome of a test. Keep in mind, however, that this chapter is not about learning the statistical procedures themselves, but rather how to be ethical and responsible in using them.

Modern statistics serve three main purposes:

- *To describe* observations about a sample using graphs and statistics (e.g., mean, standard deviation)

- *To make inferences* about a population given the statistics that describe your sample

- *To generalize* your inferences to make claims about phenomena, past or present, and make predictions about future events

Research combines all three purposes in **null-hypothesis statistical testing** (NHST), *a systematic method of using sample data to determine if there are reliable relationships* *among variables* (e.g., correlations) *or significant differences among groups* (e.g., ANOVA, as Kayla used in her example) *that are unlikely to be due to randomness in sampling or measurement.*

NHST is found in practically every peer-reviewed article in behavioral, social, and biomedical sciences and is what most faculty in these areas assume when they hear the word *statistics*. Interestingly, this has not always been the case, nor was it the original goal of those who founded the field of statistics. Members of the first professional organization related to statistics—The Royal Statistical Society— understood their role to be gathering information to share with the public, not necessarily to make inferences, generalizations, or decisions. The field may have stayed on that course; however, a couple of problems emerged. First, the mathematical developments of the discipline have placed most types of inferences and analyses well out of the reach of the general public. Second, the general public knows that statistics can be manipulated to support just about any kind of claim. The combination of these two facts places important responsibilities on those who have the knowledge and skills to use statistics in research (Pittenger, 2001). Those responsibilities are to conduct statistical tests correctly and without bias, to present honest and accurate descriptions of our methods, and to present statistics at a level of sophistication that is appropriate to our audience.

To encourage ethical practices, today's largest professional organization of statistics, the American Statistical Association (2016), has developed a comprehensive set of ethical guidelines. In psychology, organizations such as the American Psychological Association (2016, see ethics section 8.10–8.14) provide more narrowly defined ethical guidelines based on the role of statistics in research and practice.

DOMAINS OF ETHICS IN STATISTICAL PRACTICE

The most obvious ethical principle in statistics is to use real data rather than simply making up numbers. But, there is a lot more to it than that. The ASA guidelines (2016) identify eight different domains of ethics for professionals:

- *Professional Integrity and Accountability.* Ethical statisticians should work to avoid bias, take on only those projects for which they are qualified, and be open about conflicts of interest.

- *Integrity of Data and Methods.* Ethical statisticians are open and honest about the source of the data, the assumptions and methods in analyses, and limitations of the sampling, measurement, and analyses.

- *Responsibilities to Science/Public/Funder/Client.* The ethical statistician's goal is to provide honest information that is relevant to the employer's needs, not to provide the answer that the employer wants to hear.

- *Responsibilities to Research Subjects.* Ethical statisticians work only on projects in which participants are treated ethically. They store data and report results in a way that maintains anonymity and confidentiality.

- *Responsibilities to Your Research Team and Other Colleagues.* Ethical statisticians recognize that their contributions to a project will ultimately reflect on their collaborators and employers. They should be open about their practices and adapt to the standards of any discipline in which they might work.

- *Responsibilities to Other Statisticians or Statistics Practitioners.* Ethical statisticians treat collaborators and other professionals respectfully, recognizing that peer review and disagreements are part of scientific research.

- *Responsibilities Regarding Allegations of Misconduct.* Ethical statisticians understand what misconduct entails and are willing to report and investigate suspected misconduct. They will treat individuals respectfully and in a way to protect their reputation if the allegations are proven false.

- *Responsibilities of Employers.* Ethical employers will be clear about the expectations of the assigned tasks and the source and quality of data they provide. They do not pressure statisticians for answers that they want.

One reason for this breadth of categories is that professionals' work involves a wide range of organizations, can affect entire populations of individuals, and can actually impact life and death decisions. As a student, your work is not expected to have such significant consequences. Nonetheless, ethical practices relevant to students can be adapted from the ASA's guidelines. For example, in the opening to this chapter, Kayla exhibited *integrity and accountability* by seeking help when needed. She exhibited *integrity of data and methods* by openly sharing her data and allowing others to analyze it.

In the following sections, we will adapt the guidelines presented above to better align with student research and gather them into three categories. In doing so, we will review the nature of the ethics, consequences of violating them, and then make recommendations for your work.

RESPONSIBLE USE AND REPORTING OF DATA AND METHODOLOGY

The past five to 10 years have brought a dramatic increase in attention to the use of NHST. One should expect this in the editorials and commentary of general science publications such as *American Scientist* (Gelman & Loken, 2014). However, many scientists would never have predicted that discussions of statistics and scientific methodology would appear in nonscientific journalism, including political and cultural magazines such as *Newsweek* (Firger, 2015) and *The Atlantic* (Yong, 2016). This widespread interest emphasizes the responsibility of researchers not just to each other, but to the public that relies on their statistical expertise.

At the core of the discussions about NHST is the **replication crisis**, *the concern among a number of scientists (led by psychologists) that many—perhaps even most—peer-reviewed studies cannot be reproduced by other researchers.* This concern has been amplified by a widespread, coordinated effort among psychologists to replicate 100 studies sampled from three high-impact journals—an effort that resulted in less than a 40% successful replication rate (Open Science Collaboration, 2015). In other words, there are a lot of well-trained researchers facing a situation that is in some ways like Kayla's.

Before addressing the ethical side of statistical analysis, there are two important notes: First, the replication crisis is not necessarily all bad. Instead, it should be seen as an opportunity to improve science practices as a whole. Second, psychology is not alone; in fact, surveys of scientists in physical, earth, and life sciences indicate that a majority of researchers in any discipline have failed to replicate others' findings at least once. Even in sciences that are traditionally viewed as the most reliable such as physics and chemistry, over half of all surveyed researchers have failed to reproduce at least one of their own published findings (Baker, 2016).

ABUSING RESEARCHER DEGREES OF FREEDOM

Good research should be reproducible, but when a study fails to reproduce, that does not necessarily mean there are ethical problems. For example, when an experiment fails to replicate, it could be that the replication data resulted in a Type II error (i.e., failing to find an effect that really exists), or that the replication team misinterpreted some element of the procedures in the original study. These events happen because statistics is based in probability, not certainty, and humans will always be prone to mistakes. Nonetheless, there are cases in which the original authors may have fabricated the results. This type of fraud certainly happens and is clearly and purely unethical.

Between errors and mistakes on the one hand, and outright fraud on the other is a set of issues known as questionable research practices (QRPs; John et al., 2012), which were first introduced in Chapter 7. Many QRPs are based entirely within the decisions made during statistical analyses—these particular QRPs are frequently referred to as *p-hacking*. The term *p-hacking* refers to the fact that researchers hope to find a *p* value (the probability of Type I error) below .05, at which point they can claim statistical significance. To get that low level of probability, many researchers *hack*—they find ways to take advantage of—all the choices one can make when analyzing data. These **researcher degrees of freedom** *include an array of choices that are made to increase the likelihood of achieving significant results* (Simmons, Nelson, & Simonsohn, 2011). The majority of choices implicated in *p*-hacking are listed below. Just to be clear, at best these are questionable actions, but at worst, they are blatant misuse of statistics.

- Increase your sample size. If that does not quite work, increase your sample again, and then again until your reach significance.

- Measure multiple dependent variables in your study, and test each one separately. The more variables you try, the more likely you are to get significance.

- Remove individuals who are outliers. Perhaps an outlier is anyone three standard deviations away from the mean. If that does not help, try removing anyone 2.5 standard deviations from the mean.

- Restart your study with one slight change in measurement that you know will improve your outcome, but neglect to report that the original study did not work as you had hoped.

- Round down your *p* value from .059 to .05, but then claim the actual *p* value was at or below .05.

- If you find something statistically significant that you did not expect, you can create an explanation for it and claim it was one of your hypotheses.

- Worst of all, whichever techniques you take advantage of, do not report them in your paper or presentation. In other words, report only the sample size you wound up analyzing, the specific dependent variables you wound up keeping, the covariate if you decide to use it, and so on.

To reiterate, these *p*-hacking methods all take advantage of legitimate research decisions, but they become QRPs when done selectively in service of finding significant results rather than honestly testing a hypothesis. This is exactly what Kayla has done with her study, as described in the chapter opening. In her case, she was just following the steps that had been modeled for her—her professor certainly could have prepared her better for her analysis.

As described in Chapter 7, it is generally assumed among professional researchers that QRPs are commonplace (John et al., 2012), and there is statistical evidence to support those beliefs. Those who study the use of QRPs have found many examples of them, such as a series of studies in which the authors use identical dependent variables in each paper, but use different definitions and cutoff points for outliers. They have found literature reviews that documented use of multiple dependent variables, even though they were selectively omitted in the original publication. In both types of cases, the most likely explanation is *p*-hacking: The authors selected outliers and which dependent variables to present based on what supports their predictions (Franco, Malhotra, & Simonovits, 2016; John et al., 2012; Simmons et al, 2011).

Before arguing that these practices should all be eliminated, it is important to understand that researchers need to be able to find statistical significance, and good research practices help do that. Ethical issues arise, to a large extent, from **underreporting**, *the fact that the vast majority of data that scientists collect and analyze are never reported in publications or presentations.* Underreporting means that we find out only about hypotheses that seem to work, not those that fail; our knowledge is limited to what can be published. Although this is a problem for science in general, it is not necessarily an ethical problem. However, *selective underreporting* does have an ethical component. This occurs when significant findings allow a study to get published or presented, but other data from the same study are selectively left out because they are not significant or perhaps seem to contradict the researchers' hypotheses. One recent study of published articles in high-impact science journals found that 72% of the articles did not report all of the statistical comparisons or other tests that would be reasonable to conduct, given the description of the methods of the research (Franco et al., 2016). As you might expect, underreporting was far more likely when the finding was nonsignificant; this suggests that most unreported results are selectively omitted from publication.

RECOMMENDATIONS FOR STATISTICAL ANALYSIS

Many QRPs are not always questionable; they can be statistically useful and ethical practices when they are planned, open, and reproducible. Therefore, the recommendations are not just prohibitions, but advice on their proper use. For example, large sample sizes reduce error variability in estimates of means, standard deviations, and other statistics. Knowing this is useful if you plan in advance and make predictions, but it undermines the logic of NHST if you continue to adjust your sample size during research, stopping only when you achieve significance. The logic behind NHST is beyond the scope of the book but, in short, there are honest and fair ways to use sample size to your advantage. Other QRPs are in a similar situation. It is perfectly OK to select one of several, possible dependent variables before you collect data, but it is questionable to do so afterwards.

Determine your sample size in advance. From a purely statistical perspective, it would make sense to base your sample size on a **power analysis,** *a technique for calculating the optimal sample size* (see Additional Resources for more information). If you are conducting a project independently, you may not have the same access to participants as a professional, in which case you may choose to report a power analysis, even if you wind up setting a lower sample size based on your resources.

Preregister your methods. In addition to sample size, you should be able to state all hypotheses, what constitutes an outlier, the analyses you will run, and any other factors that might tempt you into QRPs. **Preregistration** occurs *when a researcher shares the full research plan, including decisions about researcher degrees of freedom, publically and prior to data collection* (Nosek & Lakens, 2014). Anyone can preregister their research online at the Open Science Foundation, which will be described in the next section of this chapter. Although for students completing smaller projects, preregistration can be as simple as sharing your data analysis plan with your peers and faculty mentor. This is often required in a research proposal.

Describe effects of outliers and covariates. If you report the results with and without a covariate, it is actually more informative to your audience or readers, and you will be writing in a more ethical way.

Post your data. If you present your research at a conference or even have the chance to publish it, include an author note that indicates a website where others can access your data or an email address so they may request it (Simonsohn, 2013). Ideally, data that are presented will be stored for at least five years. Some institutions even have a digital repository for completed capstone projects or senior theses; it would be great to include a spreadsheet of your data when submitting your final paper.

Other statistical practices. In general, you should approach your analysis knowing the NHST techniques based on certain assumptions: hypotheses will be determined in advance, data will fit a certain distribution (e.g., a normal curve), and so on. Many of these assumptions can be undermined or manipulated by p-hacking, whether it is done consciously or not, in ways that can skew or misrepresent the truth. To be safe, here are a few final recommendations to help you avoid an ethical issue:

- Employ only techniques for which you are qualified. Your mentor should be aware of how much statistical training you have completed. You should identify the analysis you plan to use before you begin your research project.

- Choose descriptive statistics, visual representations, and statistical tests that are appropriate to your data. Remember that two statistics measuring the same thing (e.g., the mean and the median both measure central tendency) can actually be quite different. There can also be large differences in the outcomes of independent versus dependent t-tests and ANOVAs.

- Identify possible sources of error in the data that might not be part of the actual statistical test. For example, imagine you are using an electronic device to measure nervous system arousal and it breaks. You may not have the resources or enough volunteers to start over. In that case, you should report the equipment failure and discuss how the switch in instruments may have introduced error into your data.

THE OPEN SCIENCE FRAMEWORK

An organization known as the Center for Open Science (COS) has been encouraging researchers to follow the practices outlined above—a collection of practices known as the *open science framework*. To facilitate open science (especially preregistration, sharing research materials, and posting data), COS provides a website that anyone can join, including you as a student researcher. In addition to hosting preregistration and providing accessible storage, the COS also recognizes open science practices through a system of icons known as *badges*. These badges are colorful icons that academic journals can include with an online table of contents and alongside the title of published manuscripts to indicate which open science practices were a part of a study. Check out Additional Resources for more information on the badges.

ETHICAL RESPONSIBILITIES TO OTHERS

To this point, we have focused on the ethics of analyzing and reporting data—that is clearly where the most complex ethical issues are raised. However, statistics in psychology usually reflect real human beings, not just the abstract parameter estimates and *p* values. Therefore, we will briefly consider how our statistical practices affect others, including participants and collaborators.

Ethical researchers ensure that participants are treated in a way that adheres to the IRB-approved protocol. During statistical analysis, researchers need to continue to ensure anonymity and responsibility to the same degree as during data collection. Although it is unlikely that a statistician would ever think of revealing an individual's name, it is sometimes easy to identify someone accidentally through other indicators, such as demographics. For example, imagine a college with fewer than 1,000 students, almost exclusively traditional aged, and in a region that is not racially or ethnically diverse. Reporting a fact about a 45-year-old, who identifies as a member of an underrepresented racial group, may be every bit as revealing as stating the individual's name. It is good practice to omit any combination of identifying demographics in the following circumstances: if it includes fewer than five individuals, if the research topic is fairly benign (e.g., a study of chewing gum preferences), if there are fewer than 10 for more controversial topics (e.g., self-reports of unpopular political views), and if there are fewer than 20 if you are addressing very highly sensitive information (e.g., criminal behavior).

Ethics related to collaborators is also important. Your work is likely to represent a joint effort; and, if you are collaborating with peers, your conduct can affect the education and professional development of others. Your conduct will also reflect on your mentor. For both types of relationships, you should address all of the ethical issues described above to avoid tarnishing the reputation of those who are helping you. Collaborators and mentors should also be involved in determining authorship and author order, as described in Chapter 3.

One of the most interesting facts about statistics is that much of what you have read here—specifically, the idea of questionable research practices—has never received much attention from an ethical perspective. This is the case even in the education and development of young scientists. Statistics textbooks, where the topics we refer to as researcher degrees of freedom, are introduced and explained individually across a series of chapters. Although research methods textbooks touch on issues of data falsification and outright fraud, the nuances of p-hacking are rarely explored in much detail. Finally, as was the case in Kayla's story, many students pick up these tricks just being immersed in a research laboratory with a professor. In all cases, there are perfect opportunities to frame QRPs as an ethical issue; but, instead, many people have come to view them as legitimate ways of getting answers out of data. At best, these might be viewed as methodological problems. However, as the publications cited in the text indicate, researchers are willfully misrepresenting their data through p-hacking and underreporting. For students of psychology, we hope that you will plan your data collection and analysis in advance, making sure to stick to your plan and reporting all relevant data.

Chapter Summary

- The ASA provides eight domains of statistical ethics. These guide researchers to think about the decisions they make when managing, analyzing, and reporting data, along with the responsibilities they have to other groups and individuals.

- There is concern of a replication crisis in psychology and many other disciplines. The low rates of replication may result, in part, from relaxed standards in conducting and reporting statistical analyses.

- Hypothesis testing is based on a set of decisions, which establish criteria for statistical significance. When used openly and honestly, NHST can be a useful tool.

- The set of QRPs known as p-hacking can use those decisions as opportunities to support one's ideas at the expense of statistical accuracy.

- The Open Science Framework is one approach to improve the quality and replicability of science.

Discussion Questions

1. Review the section **Recommendations for Statistical Practice** to make sure you understand the five main recommendations. Next, turn to Kayla's story on the first page of this chapter. Is it possible that any of those recommendations might have prevented Kayla's predicament? Explain how.

2. As you read this scenario, try to imagine what the student is thinking about as he completes his project.

Stefan's experiment seemed to take forever; he had to set up and calibrate EEG equipment and then gather baseline recordings before the study even began. He invested 18 hours of time the first week just to complete data collection with 15 participants. Although he knew he should have closer to 30 participants, he couldn't help but run a quick analysis to see how the results were coming along. The data produced interesting results with p = .095. Stefan knew that larger sample sizes produce smaller p values, everything else held constant. Based on that, he added an additional five participants and found p = .072, another three participants and got .071, and finally, with two additional participants, he reached p = .054 and decided to round that down to .05. When writing his Methods section the following week, he described the participants as "25 students from an introductory psychology course . . ." saying nothing about the fact that the test was conducted with 15 students, then 20, then 23, and finally 25.

The work was obviously very time-consuming, so most people can understand why Stefan would want to take a shortcut. How is his approach a questionable research practice? What is a more ethical approach to data collection?

3. In most of the preceding chapters of this book, we have explored ethical principles that have been developed with professional researchers in mind. In most cases, we find that the principles may need to be adapted to fit the experience level of the student researcher. With statistics, that might not be the case. Review the list of QRPs used in p-hacking and the recommendations for ethical practice. As you read this, think about whether students should follow the same, more relaxed, or more strict guidelines than those described in this chapter. Using the PASA model, what adaptations might be appropriate for student projects?

Additional Resources

American Statistical Association (ASA)

The ASA is the largest professional organization related to statistics. The main website provides links to a wide variety of resources, including information specifically for students (see the Education and the Your Career sections). The ASA provides a free booklet, *Ethical Guidelines for Statistical Practice*, which you can download in pdf format at the second link provided below.

http://www.amstat.org/

http://www.amstat.org/asa/files/pdfs/EthicalGuidelines.pdf

Center for Open Science (COS)

The COS operates with the mission to "increase openness, integrity, and reproducibility of research." The center supports this mission by hosting preregistered reports, promoting open science badges, providing training, and other services.

General website: https://cos.io/

Description of badges and evidence on their effects:

https://cos.io/our-services/open-science-badges/

Open Science Framework (OSF)

This site, maintained by the COS, helps organize research projects from beginning to end, with an emphasis on collaboration and making your research public. When you create a free account, you can share your own work and search for ongoing projects from other researchers with similar interests. To get a brief overview, watch the video on the OSF home page.

https://osf.io/

Power Calculations

To avoid *p*-hacking with sample sizes, it is a good idea to determine your sample size before data collection begins. The procedures for power analysis can be complicated at times, but with the use of an online calculator and some advice from a mentor, you can definitely improve the strength of your research. There are many options online, but this one is particularly useful and accessible: http://powerandsamplesize.com

References

American Psychological Association. (2016). *Ethical principles of psychologists and code of conduct*. Retrieved from http://www.apa.org/ethics/code/

American Statistical Association. (2016). *Ethical guidelines for statistical practice*. Retrieved from http://www.amstat.org/asa/files/pdfs/EthicalGuidelines.pdf

Baker, M. (2016). 1,500 scientists lift the lid on reproducibility. *Nature, 533*, 452–454. Retrieved from https://www.nature.com/news/1-500-scientists-lift-the-lid-on-reproducibility-1.19970

Firger, J. (2015). Science's reproducibility problem: 100 psych studies were tested and only half held up. *Newsweek*. Retrieved from http://www.newsweek.com/reproducibility-science-psychology-studies-366744

Franco, A., Malhotra, N., & Simonovits, G. (2016). Underreporting in psychology experiments: Evidence from a study registry. *Social Psychological and Personality Science, 7*, 8–12.

Gelman, A., & Loken, E. (2014). The statistical crisis in science. *American Scientist, 102*, 460.

John, L. K., Loewenstein, G., & Prelec, D. (2012). Measuring the prevalence of questionable research practices with incentives for truth telling. *Psychological Science, 23*, 524–532.

Nosek, B. A., & Lakens, D. (2014). Registered reports: A method to increase the credibility of published results. *Social Psychology, 45*, 137–141.

Open Science Collaboration. (2015). Estimating the reproducibility of psychological science. *Science, 349*(6251), aac4716.

Pittenger, D. (2001). Hypothesis testing as a moral choice. *Ethics & Behavior, 11,* 151–162.

Simmons, J. P., Nelson, L. D., & Simonsohn, U. (2011). False-positive psychology: Undisclosed flexibility in data collection and analysis allows presenting anything as significant. *Psychological Science, 22,* 1359–1365.

Simonsohn, U. (2013). Just post it: The lesson from two cases of fabricated data detected by statistics alone. *Psychological Science, 24,* 1875–1888.

Yong, E. (2016). Psychology's replication crisis can't be wished away. *The Atlantic.* Retrieved from https://www.theatlantic.com/science/archive/2016/03/psychologys-replication-crisis-cant-be-wished-away/472272/

9

ETHICAL WRITING PRACTICES

Professor Shahab was reading his student's final research report in an undergraduate experimental psychology lab course. One of the first things he noticed was that the student used many more references than was required for the literature review. Next, he noticed that the student had cited multiple primary sources in parentheses at the end of her sentences—a practice more common in graduate and professional research papers. Both observations led him to suspect plagiarism. Professor Shahab checked his suspicions with a simple web search for some of the phrases taken word for word from her paper. He quickly found a match; the student apparently had copied entire sentences and phrases verbatim from a published theoretical review. The copied text also included the citations at the end of the sentences. When confronted with her dishonesty, the student was confused about why this was wrong, stating that she had cited all of her sources.

Scientists rely on professional publications, conferences, and other venues to share their work with both the scientific community as well as the general public. In all of these cases, the readers begin with the assumption that the researcher is being accurate and honest, and, unless specifically stated, they expect the researcher to be presenting her own work. Because sharing your research is a fundamental part of science, ethical principles relevant to reporting and presenting your findings are important to understand. In this chapter, we will address the final stages of a research project—writing about your research.

We will first start with a discussion of plagiarism, and then explore the benefits of peer review during the writing process.

THE LITERATURE REVIEW

Once your research is complete, the first step in presenting your findings—whether it is a class project, conference presentation, or publication—is to provide background information for your audience. A literature review summarizes the previous research on a topic and evaluates the strengths and weaknesses of that evidence. In doing so, it provides the foundation for designing new studies or replicating and extending previous research. It is easy to become focused on supporting your own ideas, compared to finding the contradicting evidence for your hypotheses. Nonetheless, ethical writing practices require you to do both; otherwise, you will be engaging in **selective reporting**, *intentionally excluding those studies that weaken your hypotheses.*

For example, one cognitive psychology student hypothesized that studying disorganized information would lead to better learning, and she cited substantial research to support her claim. Although she found published evidence to the contrary, she decided to exclude that research from her paper, which is a typical example of selective reporting. After her mentor provided feedback on her first draft, the student decided to fix the problem by writing about the contradictory research, but then explained the contradiction on differences in the methods used by previous researchers. The difference was that a set of studies tested participants only at the end of the experimental session, and this research favored highly organized materials. In contrast, her research focused on long-term retention, including follow up tests after one week. Correcting her selective reporting paid off in two ways. Not only was her final paper more closely aligned with ethical principles, but she actually made a stronger rationale for her hypothesis. As this example illustrates, deciding what to include or leave out of a paper involves both methodological and ethical decisions, which can be quite complex. For a more in-depth review of selective reporting, we have included a link to ORI's Guide to Ethical Writing in the Additional Resources section at the end of the chapter.

It is most often in the literature review that writers, whether intentional or not, plagiarize others' work. **Plagiarism**, *misrepresenting other ideas or work as one's own*, is one of the most common forms of academic dishonesty (Rettinger & Kramer, 2009). While we covered most instances of research misconduct in Chapter 7, plagiarism requires a more in-depth discussion because of both the frequency in which it occurs and the difficulty that students and faculty face when responding to it.

WHAT IS PLAGIARISM?

We have found that students new to scientific writing often think of plagiarism as a result of APA style mistakes, but plagiarism is much more than just a citation problem. Although definitions vary considerably, Fishman (2009) has proposed a comprehensive definition of plagiarism that includes the following components:

1) Uses words, ideas, or work products

2) Attributable to another identifiable person or source

3) Without attributing the work to the source from which it was obtained

4) In a situation in which there is a legitimate expectation of original authorship

5) In order to obtain some benefit, credit, or gain which need not be monetary. (p. 5)

When a student is confronted with a plagiarism accusation, the first response is often "I didn't mean to do it!" In fact, in most cases of plagiarism, students claim a lack of knowledge or understanding about what constitutes plagiarism (Granitz & Loewy, 2007). Unfortunately, just as you might tell a police officer who has stopped you that you did not know the speed limit, ignorance of the rules is not a justifiable defense. Whether intentional or not, plagiarism is considered research misconduct and often results in serious consequences.

Why might plagiarism be such an enduring problem? One explanation is that writing about research is in many ways different from the kind of writing students learn first—the kind of writing required for the humanities, such as English and history classes. Both types of writing require reading and citing the work of others, but humanities papers often use direct quotes, which are clear signals that a citation should follow. Quotes are discouraged in scientific writing, so students must think more carefully about when they should identify that an idea has come from another source. The distinction between citing a quotation versus citing an idea can be seen in two types of plagiarism as well. **Direct plagiarism**, often the result of cutting and pasting from online sources, is *taking word for word sentences and passages from another work without any acknowledgment.* This type of plagiarism is more clear cut than other forms and most students recognize and avoid it. However, students often struggle with two other ways to draw ideas from sources: summarizing and paraphrasing. *Summarizing* involves putting a writer's ideas and arguments into your own words and in a condensed version. *Paraphrasing* means that a writer has maintained some words or phrases of the original author. Students and professors alike struggle with identifying proper forms of paraphrasing, especially when specific, technical terms must be used (Roig, 2001). Paraphrasing is more challenging to do correctly and may result in **patchwork plagiarism,** *writing nearly identical to a source with only superficial changes to key words* (often relying on a thesaurus). Here is an example:

Original sentence:

"It should be noted under deontology and cultural relativism there is not necessarily an awareness of a transgression." (Granitz & Loewy, 2007, p. 298)

Patchwork plagiarism:

It should be observed under the study of wrongdoing and social contingency there is not automatically a consciousness of a misbehavior.

Not only is patchwork plagiarism stealing, it often results in rather awkward sentences that confuse readers. In this example, paraphrasing or summarizing would not just be more ethical, it would result in better writing. If you cannot clearly paraphrase or summarize an idea but feel that it is necessary to include, then you may use a direct quote and cite it properly.

As noted earlier, writers are more likely to overlook citations for summaries than for direct quotes. However, careless or accidental plagiarism is still plagiarism. The best strategy for students learning to avoid those mistakes is to get feedback while working through examples. In the Additional Resources section at the end of the chapter, we have included a link to an online tutorial on academic integrity that specifically targets plagiarism. Research indicates that completing this type of tutorial does reduce future instances of plagiarism (Dee & Jacob, 2010).

Students often think of plagiarism as the failure to cite another author, but this does not account for **self-plagiarism**, which is the *act of an author reusing his or her own previous work, in whole or in part, without properly acknowledging it.* This can take the form of written work as well as data and images and involves copying from one's previous publication. Self-plagiarism is often referred to as **double dipping**, *gaining credit twice for only one piece of work.* As students develop a program of research, especially in graduate school, they often write multiple papers on the same subject matter for a thesis, conference presentation, and publication. In this case, a writer must be deliberate in avoiding self-plagiarism because with each paper, it becomes increasingly possible to accidently use nearly the exact language. At worst, authors can engage in deliberate self-plagiarism known as **duplicate publication,** in which *an author publishes the same study or other text in two different journals.* For students who may not be ready to publish, self-plagiarism is more likely to involve submitting the same paper for two different courses. Although the paper was not published, it is using the same work to gain credit in two courses. It is considered plagiarism and is explicitly banned at some institutions.

Professional ethical guidelines state any written work, even your own, should be treated the same way when it comes to citations and references. This means you should not use sections of text that you have already published in subsequent papers without properly citing it as a quote. It is important to remember that self-plagiarism is really about copying text. It is perfectly acceptable to use ideas from previous work to design a new study or line of inquiry; in fact, this is how research should progress, with each study raising new research questions to explore. When writing a new paper, however, each previous work should be cited properly, just as any other paper would be. While the Office of Research Integrity does not consider self-plagiarism to be research misconduct, they do consider it an unethical writing practice because it involves some level of deception of the reader (Office of Research Integrity, n.d.).

WHY IS PLAGIARISM UNETHICAL?

Once instructed, students learn that the act of plagiarism is wrong, but often struggle to understand why it is unethical—especially with self-plagiarism. To clarify this, think of plagiarism as a form of academic dishonesty, such as copying from another student's exam. This is clearly academic dishonesty, but the underlying reason for calling it cheating is that the student will gain credit for work that she did not do. Further, students may earn course credit toward graduation or add a publication to their resume or CV. These achievements are meant to signal the quality of work a student can do. When a student gets their work published, it has the potential to provide opportunities and open doors, giving an unfair advantage when applying to internships, graduate schools, and jobs. The quote below from the Neuroskeptic blog (2016) sums it up well:

> Plagiarists steal opportunity from their honest peers. In science, for instance, jobs, promotions and funding are assigned largely on the basis of the publication records of the candidates. There are not enough of these things to go around. So whenever a plagiarist wins one of these prizes on the strength of their unfairly inflated record, someone else misses out.

What are the consequences of plagiarizing? Because plagiarism is considered research misconduct, it can have the same kind of penalties as those for other types of misconduct—a topic discussed in length in Chapter 7. Although institutions of higher education tend to have similar definitions of plagiarism, they identify and handle cases of plagiarism quite differently. Students should educate themselves both on how to write ethically but also on their institution's policies and procedures for handling instances of plagiarism.

Looking back at the scenario at the beginning of the chapter—what mistakes did the student make? First, it is likely that the student violated an important writing rule: Do not cite a source that you did not read. In this case, the student read a review article, and therefore should have cited it. Failing to do so is one form of plagiarism. In addition, she cited *primary sources* (i.e., the original studies referenced in the review) which she did not read; that is a second form of plagiarism. Finally, she made no attempt to summarize or paraphrase the literature review. Copying the text from the review article is a clear instance of plagiarism. Therefore, the student was charged with academic dishonesty and had to appear before the Honor Code committee. The committee determined that although she included many citations in her paper, she was actually plagiarizing summaries of that research directly and without credit to the author. After being found responsible for plagiarism, she received a failing grade on the paper and was required to rewrite the lab report integrating the sources she used with proper citations.

Penalties for plagiarism vary widely from one institution to the next. In many undergraduate programs, a student who is caught plagiarizing may receive a failing grade in a course or even suspension. For graduate students, the consequence is more likely to be expulsion. This is why it is so important for students to learn how to write ethically and with integrity before taking on a significant writing assignment. As faculty, we are always searching for sources and information to support our students' writing. One useful approach is to incorporate peer review into the writing process to help students identify and address plagiarism and other unethical writing practices.

PEER REVIEW

The work of scientists goes through peer review before it is shared publicly. **Peer review** is *the process in which scientists review a manuscript to determine if it meets the acceptable standards for presentation or publication.* Peer review is managed by journal editors or conference organizers who recruit the authors' peers—other scientists who conduct research in the same field. Reviewers critique the quality of research design, data analysis, the authors' conclusions, and whether the paper has been written clearly enough for other readers to understand it correctly. In this way, science relies on peer review to distinguish high-quality research from poorly designed studies, and research that is likely to have high impact versus that which is irrelevant to the field. Reviewers may also detect plagiarism or research misconduct, although that may not happen often (Smith, 2006). Peer review is not without its flaws (see Smith, 2006, for a review), but it remains the primary practice for reviewing studies prior to publication.

Ethical Guidelines for Peer Review

It is important to understand who peer reviewers are and why peer review can pose an ethical dilemma. A peer is someone who is at minimum a trained scientist in the field but, at best, an expert on the topic under study. In this case, a peer is not necessarily a friend or colleague, although that may sometimes be the case. When reviewers have prior relationships or contact with the authors, the peer review process itself can create a conflict of interest. One way to maintain the integrity of the review process is **blind review,** *a review in which the editor takes measures to ensure the authors and reviewers remain anonymous to one another.* To think about the value of blind review, imagine that a graduate student's research results seriously challenge an established researcher's findings. When the student submits the study for publication, the journal editor may ask the senior researcher to serve as a peer reviewer for the manuscript. This reviewer, who would have influence in the field, could then attempt to damage the student's research program by calling into question the student's integrity or work. This would obviously be unethical, but blind review greatly reduces the chance of these behaviors ever occurring.

Honesty is another important quality of peer review. In the previous example, the reviewer held a lot of influence over whether the study would be published, and had personal and professional motivations for preventing its publication. If he submits a rather scathing review of the study, the journal editor must consider whether this one reviewer has a valid, but unique perspective, or is simply being protective of his own work. Obviously, the ethical approach is to put one's feelings and personal motivations aside, and to provide an honest assessment of the manuscript. This is every bit as important when a reviewer receives a manuscript that supports and strengthens her own work. The principles above still apply; the researcher should provide a legitimate assessment.

Finally, the APA ethical principles (2016, 8.15) require that reviewers should respect the confidentiality and authorship of the material being reviewed. A reviewer may not use any material or information obtained during a peer review. For example, the reviewer should not take the methods and results from that manuscript to a conference and present it as his own.

This section illustrates how professionals use peer review to determine whether someone's work meets high enough standards to be published or presented at a conference. When done carefully and ethically, it is a very effective system. However, peer review is useful at all stages of the writing process and for research that takes other forms, such as students' papers.

Peer Review for Students

Some instructors assign peer review in their courses, and this can be an excellent learning experience (Guilford, 2001; Kennette & Frank, 2013). A peer review can be very useful for students to gain feedback on both the content of their work as well as the writing. Not only can peer review indicate how well you are communicating your ideas and following proper guidelines, it can also serve as a check for plagiarism and other issues of data analysis and presentation. And, consistent with the theme of this book, it gives a chance for peer reviewers to learn about ethics, because students who peer review each other's work should be held to the same standard as their professors. Research has even shown that reviewing a peer's paper can improve a student's own writing (Kennette & Frank, 2013). Further, practicing the peer review process increases students' understanding of how research is published (Guilford, 2001). We encourage faculty and students to incorporate some form of peer review when students are working on a research paper. We have provided additional resources related to peer review at the end of the chapter.

Chapter Summary

- Plagiarism takes many forms, including direct plagiarism, patchwork plagiarism, and self-plagiarism.

- Plagiarism is unethical because it gives an unfair advantage to the plagiarizer for jobs, future research opportunities, and potential graduate programs.

- Peer review is an essential part of the publication process and can potentially catch plagiarism.

- Students who participate in peer review activities not only improve their own writing, but also learn more about professional writing and publication.

Discussion Questions

1. A psychology student wants to use a portion of a research proposal she wrote in her research methods course as the starting point for her senior capstone project. She earned an *A* on the proposal and received constructive feedback from her instructor. Additionally, she has plenty of sources to begin her literature review. Can she reuse portions of her literature review for another class? What advice would you give her?

2. Some people view plagiarism as theft. After reading this chapter, how might you argue that it is more than just theft?

3. As you approach writing up your research findings, how might peer review help inform your ethical writing practices?

Additional Resources

Ethics and Scientific Publication

Using case studies, the authors outline the major ethical violations that can occur in scientific publication. They include a discussion of plagiarism as well as duplicate and redundant publication.

Benos, D., Fabres, J., Farmer, J., Gutierrez, J., Hennessey, K., Kosek, D., . . . Wang, K. (2005). Ethics and scientific publication. *Advances in Physiology Education, 29,* 59–74.

Northern Illinois University's Academic Dishonesty Tutorial on Plagiarism

These academic integrity tutorials for students and faculty focus on the causes and consequences of academic dishonesty, such as cheating, plagiarism, and research misconduct. The tutorial includes useful quizzes to test your knowledge.

https://www.niu.edu/academic-integrity/faculty/types/index.shtml

Office of Research Integrity's Guide to Ethical Writing

Presents a set of modules to assist both students and professors with ethical writing practices. In addition to covering different types of plagiarism, it also includes modules on selective reporting in the literature review, methods, and results.

https://ori.hhs.gov/avoiding-plagiarism-self-plagiarism-and-other-questionable-writing-practices-guide-ethical-writing

Teaching Peer Review

Guilford offers a process for peer review for students that mimics professional peer review where the instructor acts as the editor. The procedure can be adapted for any course that has a substantial writing component.

Guilford, W. H. (2001). Teaching peer review and the process of scientific writing. *Advances in Physiology Education, 25*(3), 167–175.

References

American Psychological Association. (2016). *Ethical principles of psychologists and code of conduct*. Retrieved from http://www.apa.org/ethics/code/

Dee, T., & Jacob, B. (2010). Rational ignorance in education: A field experiment in student plagiarism. *Journal of Human Resources, 47*, 397–434.

Fishman, T. (2009). "We know it when we see it" is not good enough: Toward a standard definition of plagiarism that transcends theft, fraud, and copyright, 4th Asia Pacific Conference on Educational Integrity (4APCEI), University of Wollongong NSW Australia. 28–30 September 2009. Retrieved from http://ro.uow.edu.au/cgi/viewcontent.cgi?article=1037&context=apcei

Granitz, N., & Loewy, D. (2007). Applying ethical theories: Interpreting and responding to student plagiarism. *Journal of Business Ethics, 72*, 293–306.

Guilford, W. H. (2001). Teaching peer review and the process of scientific writing. *Advances in Physiology Education, 25*, 167–175.

Kennette, L. N., & Frank, N. M. (2013). The value of peer feedback opportunities for students in writing intensive classes. *Psychology Teaching Review, 19*, 106–111.

Neuroskeptic. (2016, January 26). Plagiarism is theft—But of what? Retrieved from http://blogs.discovermagazine.com/neuroskeptic/2016/01/26/plagiarism-is-theft/# .WqAhh2rwapo

Office of Research Integrity. (n.d.). *Self-plagiarism*. Retrieved from https://ori.hhs .gov/plagiarism-13

Rettinger, D., & Kramer, Y. (2009). Situational and personal causes of student cheating. *Research in Higher Education, 50*, 293–313.

Roig, M. (2001). Paraphrasing and plagiarism criteria of college and university professors. *Ethics & Behavior, 11*, 307–323.

Smith, R. (2006). Peer review: A flawed process at the heart of science and journals. *Journal of the Royal Society of Medicine, 99*, 178–182.

INDEX